DICTIONARY
SHMICTIONARY!

DICTIONARY SHMICTIONARY!

A YIDDISH AND YINGLISH DICTIONARY

By Paul Hoffman and Matt Freedman

QUILL • NEW YORK • 1983

Library of Congress Cataloging in Publication Data

Hoffman, Paul, 1956–
Dictionary shmictionary!

1. Yiddish language—Dictionaries—English.
2. English language—Foreign words and phrases—
Yiddish—Dictionaries. I. Freedman, Matt. II. Title.
PJ5117.H65 1983   437'.947   83–3050
ISBN 0-688-02162-X (pbk.)

Printed in the United States of America

First Quill Edition

1 2 3 4 5 6 7 8 9 10

BOOK DESIGN BY LINEY LI

TO JAMES HOFFMAN

To Uncle Milton
& Aunt Bert

with love
from nephew

Matt

ACKNOWLEDGMENTS

We want to thank the following *gaons* who have contributed to this book: Barbara Cramer, Pam Diamond, Andrea Dorfman, Gail Edwards, Darlene Ehrenberg, Bobby Freedman, Dorothy Freedman, Aunt Fan Freedman, Larry Freedman, Lynn Freedman, Stuart Haber, John Himmelfarb, Jae Hoffman, James Hoffman, John Horton, Jeffrey Kluger, April Lasher, Toni Schlesinger, Judy Stone, Eva Teich, and Yuri Suhl.

Alevay there's no *bulbe, narishkeit,* or bad *tam* in *Dictionary Shmictionary!,* but if there is any, none of these people is *farant-vortlech.*

The examples for *shickery* were cited in *A Dictionary of Australian Colloquialisms* (G. A. Wilkes, Routledge & Kegan Paul, London, 1978).

Sargent Shriver's use of *kreplach* and Sid Caesar's pun on *metsieh* come from Lillian Mermin Feinsilver's wonderful book *The Taste of Yiddish* (A. S. Barnes & Company, Inc., South Brunswick, N.J., 1970).

INTRODUCTION

"I'm the *yenta* of Paradise Valley. I have introduced a number of couples, including my own sister and brother-in-law," said Justice Sandra Day O'Connor in a revealing interview with *Ladies' Home Journal* (March 1982). What Justice O'Connor revealed, however, was her ability not only to make matches but also to misuse Yiddish. The word for matchmaker in Yiddish is *shadchen; yenta* means "blabbermouth" or "nag." Perhaps the Justice was confused because the *shadchen* in *Fiddler on the Roof* has the name Yente.

"Chutzpah" was the lead headline of a December 1980 issue of the Hearst newspaper the *Boston Herald American.* The accompanying article chronicled the shamelessly audacious style of Boston Mayor Kevin White. The article correctly defined *chutzpah* as "brass," but erroneously described it as an "American colloquialism," with no mention of Yiddish. What nerve!

You're in pretty elite company then if you don't know much about Yiddish. This book, *Dictionary Shmictionary,* provides pronunciations, etymologies, definitions, and example sentences of Yiddish words and Yinglish words (bastardized Yiddishisms) that have infiltrated English. Yiddish words have been spoken and written in American English since the Colonial days, but in the past two and a half decades, they have shown up, sometimes inappropriately, in the most gentile of contexts. In 1957 when super-WASP Queen Elizabeth announced her plans to travel to New York City, the *New York Post* reported that "Queen Elizabeth will *schlep* along 95 pieces of baggage on her trip here." On January 12, 1968, when student radicals were taking over university buildings, *The Wall Street Journal* ran the headline "Revolution, Shmevolution."

In 1975 Yiddish even made the Harvard student newspaper. In Cambridge, Massachusetts, a fierce squabble had broken out among tenants, landlords, politicians, and Harvard University administrators over proposed changes in the city's housing code. The debate raged for weeks, with each interest group complaining that the others were ignoring the needs of some hard-pressed segment of the population. The *Harvard Crimson* ran a story with the headline "Cambridge Kvetches."

Yiddish words are common not only in newspapers and magazines but also in novels, short stories, movies, musicals, TV skits, and political statements. *Dictionary Shmictionary!* includes Yiddish words used by people you'd think would use them; namely, Woody Allen, Menachem Begin, Saul Bellow, Mel Brooks, Lenny Bruce, Sid Caesar, Abraham Cahan, Al Capp, Leslie Fiedler, Sigmund Freud, Joseph Heller, Ed Koch, Bernard Malamud, S. J. Perelman, Henry Roth, Barbra Streisand, Yuri Suhl, Calvin Trillin, and Jerome Weidman. But the book also contains many colorful examples from unexpected sources: Richard Nixon, Charles Dickens, the Rolling Stones, Sargent Shriver, Johnny Carson, Bob Hope, Ann Landers, Jack London, John Updike, William Styron, and Kurt Vonnegut, Jr.

Isaac Bashevis Singer once pointed out that Yiddish is probably the only language in the world that has not been spoken among people in power. Every other known language has been used by the men and women who governed a country or the chiefs who led a tribe. (Even in Israel, Yiddish is scarcely spoken at official functions because until recently it was dismissed as the vulgar tongue of the uneducated masses, vastly inferior to the Hebrew language of Scripture.) Nonetheless, in Washington, at least, individual Yiddish words and phrases are rolling off the tongues of high-level officials. Yiddish has crept into the Pentagon as well as the Supreme Court. In 1967 a senior military strategist described to *Newsweek* the geometric pattern of the American air offensive against Haiphong: "You might call it the *bagel* strategy." And Richard Nixon can be heard on the White House tapes saying, "That's not *kosher.*"

It is not surprising that Yiddish words are found in American fiction about Jewish immigrants who live on the Lower East Side of New York, but why are the words also widely used elsewhere in English? For one thing, the words sound wonderful. Indeed, many are virtually onomatopoeic. Does not the sound of *kvetch* suggest whining and carping? And the strong gutturalness of *chutzpa* suggest unmitigated gall?

Even in fiction that does not involve Judaism or Jews, it is not uncommon for American writers to base the names of their characters on robust, humorous-sounding Yiddish words. S. J. Perelman was the champion of such names. He created, in "Looking for Pussy," the Honorable Auberon Rachmonnies (*rachmones* is Yiddish for "compassion") and introduced, in "Methinks the Lady Doth Propel Too Much," the physically unimpressive Professor Pitzel ("Professor Penis"), who is busy grafting eyes onto salamanders that have not seen the light of day for two hundred million years. Calvin Trillin, in his humor column in *The Nation*, said that the top man in the Bank of England was "the daft but wily Lord Boode of Gelt" (*gelt* is Yiddish for "money").

Such constructed names are also found, surprisingly, in science fiction. In Stanley Weinbaum's "A Martian Odyssey," there is an engineer named Putz ("Penis"), who when he is speaking is sometimes described as "ejaculating." The practice of using Yiddish words as names is by no means restricted to people. For example, Perelman, in "Misty Behind the Curtain," mentions the ship the S.S. *Pascudnik* (the S.S. *Odious*).

One of the beauties of Yiddish, which American writers have caught onto, is that the same word can be used to express opprobrium in one context and admiration in another. Such is the case with *shaygets,* an ethnic slur for a non-Jewish male, which comes from the Hebrew for "disgusting because uncircumcised." *Shaygets,* however, does not always mean a revolting gentile. It can also mean a handsome lad of any religious persuasion who charms the pants off women. "I couldn't resist him. He's such a *shaygets,*" a Jewish woman might say.

Pisher is another Yiddish word that has more than one face. The word literally means someone who urinates, and comes from the German verb *pissen.* When applied to an adult, *pisher* is a crude way of saying that the person is inconsequential—a nobody. The word has essentially the same meaning when it is applied to inanimate objects. Helen Bober, in Bernard Malamud's *The Assistant,* turns down Louis Karp's marriage proposal because she doesn't want a storekeeper for a husband. Karp responds, "Wines and liquors aren't exactly *pisher* groceries." The word *pisher* also figures in the defiant command *"Ruf mich pisher"* (Literally, "Call me pisser"), which means "Say what you will. Sticks and stones may break my bones but names will never hurt me." When applied to a child, however, *pisher* is a term of great endearment. Many a male infant has been affectionately addressed as *pisherel* ("little squirt"). And if you met a woman and asked her how many children she has, she might reply: "Three. One in nursery school and two *pishers.*"

The appearance of *pisher* in a wide variety of contexts brings out an aspect of Yiddish that the squeamish find disturbing: the frequent reference to urological, scatological, and sexual products and acts. Witness the common advice *Kak im um* ("Crap on him"), which means "Get revenge." To Yiddish speakers such expressions are not at all vulgar but earthy or even wholesome. Many of them have been uttered for eight centuries. It should be kept in mind that Judaism, unlike many other major religions, has never treated sex and most other bodily functions as disgusting. In fact, Hebrew teachings express wonderment at the spectacular workings of all the orifices of the human body, observing that man would not exist if God closed any opening or opened any closed part. Although the Talmud prohibits adultery and has a hands–off attitude toward menstruation, it encourages a couple to have frequent intercourse in whatever position they please. "A man may have sexual relations with his wife in any manner he prefers. It is the same as in eating meat. Some like it roasted, some salted, some sodden." As a result of this kind of sanctioned permissiveness, Yiddish has a rich vocabulary of amusing words for every mucous membrane.

Yiddish began as the language of exiled Jews. Like most European languages, it developed about a thousand years ago when Jewish emigrants from France and Italy settled in the Rhine basin. The settlers learned to speak the Middle High German of the Rhineland, to which they added bits and pieces of the languages they brought with them: Loez (Jewish vernaculars of Old French and Old Italian), Hebrew, and Aramaic (the vernacular of the Near East and the Middle East). In the twelfth century this polyglot German, which was to become Yiddish, flourished in the ghettos. From the beginning Yiddish was written with Hebrew characters because Jews despised the Christian overtones of

the Latin alphabet. In the twelfth, the thirteenth, and the four-
teenth centuries, the Crusades and the Black Death drove the Jews
from the Rhineland to Poland, Lithuania, and Russia. There
Yiddish picked up words from Slavic tongues. The pogroms of
the late nineteenth and early twentieth centuries forced the Jews
to emigrate from Poland and Russia to Western Europe, the
United States, and South America. Again Yiddish took on words
from the local languages.

It is estimated that about 70 percent of the prefixes, suffixes,
and root words of Yiddish come from German, 20 percent from
Hebrew, and 10 percent from Slavic tongues and other languages.
Some Yiddish words are derived from all three sources. Take
schlimazalnik, referring to a person who always brings bad
luck. *Schlimazalnik* comes from the German *schlimm* (bad), the
Hebrew *mazal* (luck), and the Slavic *nik* (for an ardent practitioner of).

The fact that Yiddish is traditionally written with the Hebrew alphabet means that when Yiddish words have been rend-
ered into English, they have been spelled every which way. The
YIVO Institute, which is for Yiddish what the *Académie Française*
is for French, has developed a system for spelling Yiddish words
phonetically in English. Unfortunately, the system has not caught
on. In *Dictionary Shmictionary!* the main entry for each word
appears under what we consider to be the most common English
spelling, however phonetically apt or barbaric it may be. Alternative spellings are also listed alphabetically, however, with a cross-
reference to the main entry; consequently, you will find a word
in *Dictionary Shmictionary!* even if you look it up under an
uncommon spelling.

A Yiddish word may be pronounced in more ways than one
depending on where in the world it is spoken. The pronunciations given in *Dictionary Shmictionary!* are based on what we have
heard. To make the book as accessible as possible, we have not
used diacritical marks. All you need to know is that the syllables
written with capital letters are accented, and that the combination
kh is pronounced gutturally like the *ch* in Bach or "*Achtung!*"

DICTIONARY
SHMICTIONARY!

AHNTOISHUNG

Pronounced "on-TOY-shung." From the German *Enttäuschung,* "disappointment."
Noun: disappointment.

> Many Yiddish proverbs warn that the price of present joy may be future *ahntoishung* or much worse. Example: "If you dance at every wedding, you'll weep at every death."

A.K.   See *alter kocker.*

ALEICHEM SHALOM   See *shalom aleichem.*

ALEVAI   See *alevay.*

ALEVAY

Also *alevai, halevai,* and *halevay.* Pronounced "olive-EYE" or "hal-ive-EYE." From the Hebrew *al'vay,* "may it be so."
Exclamation: I wish it were so; would that it were so; would that it would come true.

> *Alevay* is generally used in contexts in which what is wished for probably won't turn out to be the case. *Alevay* is a good choice to replace the overused, grammatically incorrect "hopefully."

ALMONA   See *almone.*

ALMONE

Also *almona* and *almoona.* Pronounced "oll-MOON-eh" or "AL-moan-eh." From the Hebrew *almanah,* "widow."
Noun: a widow.

There is much truth to the Yiddish proverb "When someone comforts a young *almone,* he doesn't mean to do good." Witness this confession to "A Bintel Brief" ("A Bundle of Letters"), a serious and poignant forerunner of "Dear Abby" in the *Jewish Daily Forward,* a Yiddish working-class newspaper published on New York's Lower East Side. In 1906 an *almone* wrote: "I have a grievous wound in my heart and maybe through the 'Bintel Brief' I will find relief. I am a young woman. I was happily married, but a year ago death suddenly took my husband. . . . In the carriage on the way to the cemetery I sat in a daze. My daughter and a young man, my husband's best friend, were with me. When they covered my husband's coffin I became hysterical, screamed and tried to stop them. . . . My husband's friend didn't leave my side. . . . The friend was not as handsome, well built or attractive as my husband, and he had never shown the least interest in me as a woman. . . . I don't know how it happened that during the drive home from the cemetery I was alone in the carriage with my husband's friend. . . ." You can figure out the rest.

ALMOONA   See *almone.*

ALRIGHTNICK   See *alrightnik.*

YOUNG DR. ALRIGHTNIK

ALRIGHTNIK

Also *alrightnick* and *olreitnik.* Pronounced "all-RIGHT-nick." See the entry for *-nik.*

1. Noun: someone who has risen from rags to riches—and lets everyone know it.
2. Noun: "one of us"; someone who's OK for your daughter to go out with.

> "They moved again, to Brooklyn, where Harriet fell in love with young Dr. Wolff, an *alrightnik* with soft brown eyes and an appetite for excellence who was attracted to the sixteen-year-old girl's soft good humor" (Geoffrey Wolff, *The Duke of Deception*).

ALTER COCKER   See *alter kocker.*

ALTER KOCKER
Also *A.K.* and *alter cocker.* Pronounced "ALL-ter-COCK-er." From the German *alter,* "old," and *Kocker,* "crapper." Literally, "old crapper."
1. Noun: an old fart; a crotchety, fidgety old man; a fuddy-duddy.
2. Noun: a lecherous old man.
3. Noun *(A.K.):* a has-been.

> *Variety,* the magazine of the entertainment world, is chiefly responsible for the popularity of *A.K.* in American English. Years ago *Variety,* with its tongue firmly in its cheek, maintained that *A.K.* stood for "antediluvian knight"; certain gullible wordsmiths have perpetuated this definition not in jest but in complete seriousness! In England *A.K.* stands for "ass kisser." (In Yiddish *T.L.* is reserved for that concept.)

AM HA-ARETZ   See *amorets.*

AMHO'ORETS   See *amorets.*

AMHORETZ   See *amorets.*

AMORETS
Also *am ha-aretz, amho'orets,* and *amhoretz.* Pronounced "am-HOR-ets." From the Hebrew *am haaretz,* "people of the land."
1. Noun: a peasant; an illiterate and uneducated person.

> "That was Lazansky, in the bakery, a giant teamster from the Ukraine. A huge important man, an *amhoretz* who didn't know enough Hebrew to bless his bread" (Saul Bellow, *Herzog*).

2. Noun: an ignoramus.

> The Talmud says, "Talking sense to an *amorets* is like describing music to a deaf man, a rainbow to a blind man, and the pleasures of sex to a eunuch." There is a Yiddish proverb: "One *amorets* can ask more questions than ten wise men can answer." In spite of these harsh words, the tolerance of ignorance in Judaism is a double-edged sword; there is another Yiddish proverb: "Don't ridicule the *amorets* because you might be denouncing your own ancestors."

APIKOROS

Also *apikoyres*. Pronounced "eh-pah-KAY-ress." From the Hebrew *apikoros*, based on the name of the Greek hedonistic philosopher Epicurus. The plural of *apikoros* is *apikorsim*.
1. Noun: a hedonist.
2. Noun: an unbeliever; an atheist.

> "It's tough to be an *apikoros* because you don't get any days off."

> "Dov Shlomowitz came up to the plate. He stood like a bear, the bat looking like a matchstick in his beefy hands. Schwartzie pitched, and he sliced one neatly over the head of the third baseman for a single. The Yeshiva team howled, and one of them called out to us in Yiddish, "Burn, you *apikorsim!*" and Sidney Goldberg and I looked at each other without saying a word" (Chaim Potok, *The Chosen*).

APIKORSIM   See *apikoros*.

APIKOYRES   See *apikoros*.

AROYSGEVORFENEH

Also *aroysgevorfine*. Pronounced "ah-ROYCE-ge-vor-fen-eh." From the German *abwerfen*, "to cast off."
Adjective: discarded; wasted.

> In Yiddish there is a common expression, *aroysgevorfeneh gelt*, "wasted money."

AROYSGEVORFINE   See *aroysgevorfeneh*.

ARUMGEFLICKT

ARUMGEFLICKT

Pronounced "a-ROOM-ge-FLICKT." From the German *pflücken*, "to pluck," as in feathers. Literally, "plucked."
Adjective: fleeced.

ARUMSCHLEPPEN

ARUMLOIFER

Pronounced "a-ROOM-loy-fer." From the German *loifen,* "to run."
Literally, "someone who runs around."
Noun: a street urchin.

> Everyone is familiar with the greatest *arumloifers* in history: Little
> Orphan Annie, Oliver Twist, and O. J. Simpson.

ARUMSCHLEPPEN

Also *arumshleppen.* Pronounced "a-ROOM-shlep-en." From the Yiddish
schleppen, "to drag."
Verb: to have a pointless relationship; to go out with someone with no
possibility of anything "meaningful" developing. Everybody's experienced this. The less said, the better.

ARUMSHLEPPEN   See *arumschleppen.*

AVERAH

Also *aveyre.* Pronounced "a-VAY-rah." From the Hebrew *averah,* "sin."
Noun: a sin.

> An old Yiddish adage says: "It's an *averah* to throw it out."

AVEYRE   See *averah.*

BAGEL

Pronounced "BAY-gull." Perhaps from the German *Beugel* (*Baug-* is a German prefix for "ring"), "stirrup."
Noun: a hard, doughnut-shaped roll that is boiled before it is baked. *Bagels* come in many flavors: plain, onion, whole wheat, poppy seed, pepper, cinnamon, raisin, and so on.

> "I really love *bagel* and lox," a WASP told Shlomo. "But do tell me—which is the *bagel* and which is the lox?"

> In 1967 a senior Pentagon strategist described to *Newsweek* the geometric pattern of the American air offensive against Haiphong: "You might call it the *bagel* strategy."

> "May you lie in the earth and bake *bagels*" is an old Yiddish curse.

BAITSIM

Also *beytsim*. Pronounced "BAIT-sum." From the Hebrew *beytsim*, "eggs."
1. Noun: eggs.

> "It's a bad idea to put all your *baitsim* in one basket."

2. Noun: testicles.

> Moshe found a genie in his *shnaps* bottle. "I'll grant you three wishes," said the magus, "but I must warn you that whatever I give you, I'm going to give double to your neighbor Shlomo." This presented Moshe with a dilemma, for of all the people in the world he hated no one more than Shlomo. But instant gratification Moshe could not pass up.
> "All my life," he told the genie, "I've wanted to live in a mansion with twenty-four rooms, six bathrooms, and eight closets."

"Done," said the sorcerer. No sooner had Moshe's dream house materialized out of thin air than a forty-eight-room, twelve-bathroom, sixteen-closet mansion appeared in Shlomo's yard. Moshe shuddered.

"What's your second wish?" the genie asked.

"Well, all my life I've been a lonely man and I've always wanted to have a voluptuous woman waiting for me in every room of my house." *Boiing!* Instantly, two dozen beautiful women appeared in the windows, screaming his name. Next door, however, forty-eight women materialized, calling out Shlomo's name. Moshe was silent.

"Your third wish, master?"

Moshe did not answer for five minutes. Suddenly a smile crossed his face, and he said: "Genie, cut off one of my *baitsim*!"

3. (Vulgar) noun (*beytsemer*): a disparaging word for an Irishman.

BALABUSTA   See *baleboste*.

BALAGOLEH

Also *balegole*. Pronounced "ba-la-GO-leh." From the Hebrew *baal agulah*, "coachman."
Noun: a vulgar person.

BALBATIM

Also *balebatim*. Pronounced "bol-BOT-im." From the Hebrew *ba'al habayit*, "master of the house."
Noun: a boss; a leader.

BALBATISHEH   See *balebatish*.

BALEBATIM   See *balbatim*.

BALEBATISH

Also *balbatisheh* (female). Pronounced "bol-BOT-ish-(eh)." From the Hebrew *ba'al habayit*, "master of the house."
Adjective: honorable.

"Yetta, I had come to learn, was deep down a good egg, or, in the other idiom, a *balbatisheh* lady" (William Styron, *Sophie's Choice*).

BALEBOOSTEH   See *baleboste*.

BALEBOS   See *baleboss*.

BALEBOSS
Also *balebos*. Pronounced "bol-uh-BOOS." From the Hebrew *ba'al haba-yit*, "master of the house."
Noun: a male owner, boss, or head of household.

We know of a professor at the University of Wisconsin who taught freshman English to four hundred students. On the final exam the students were asked to analyze two poems, an unidentified Shakespearean sonnet and an anonymous little ditty, "Democracy in the Shoestore Window," which the professor had secretly written especially for the exam. The theme of the anonymous poem was driven home by the refrain "The workers' shoes and *baleboss*'s shoes all lined up in a row." To the professor's horror virtually all the students thought "Democracy in the Shoestore Window" was the superior poem because it was "socially relevant."

BALEBOSTE
Also *balabusta* and *baleboosteh*. Pronounced "bol-uh-BOOS-tuh." From the Hebrew ba'al *habayit*, "master of the house."
1. Noun: a woman who keeps a fastidious household.
2. Noun: a bossy, overbearing woman.

"A Jewish American Princess is . . . the guru of Gucci, the sultan of Sasson, the *baleboste* of Bergdorf's and the lord of Taylor" (from the record *The Jewish American Princess*).

There is a restaurant in Berkeley, California, called *Balabusta*.

BALEBOSTEVEN
Pronounced "bol-eh-BOOS-te-ven." From the Yiddish *baleboste*, "fastidious homemaker."
Verb: to bustle like a meticulous housewife.

BALEGOLE   See *balagoleh*.

BALMALOCHA

Also *balmelokhe.* Pronounced "bal-me-LUH-kheh." From the Hebrew *ba'al melakha,* "craftsman."
Noun: a connoisseur. Often used sarcastically.

BALMECHULE

Pronounced "bal-me-KHOOL-uh." From the Hebrew *ba'al,* "one who does," and the Yiddish *mechuleh,* "failed."
(Garment-worker slang) noun: a bad worker.

BALMELOKHE   See *balmalocha.*

BANDIT   See *bonditt.*

BANDITT   See *bonditt.*

BAR MITZVAH

Pronounced "bar-MITS-vuh." From the Aramaic *bar,* "son," and the Hebrew *mitzvah,* "commandment." Literally, "son of the commandment."
Noun: a ceremony in which a boy of thirteen or older is accepted as a member of the adult religious community.

BATLAN

Pronounced "BOT-lin." From the Hebrew *botl,* "void."
1. Noun: an idler; a nonperson. Originally someone who was unemployed and therefore always available to complete a *minyan,* or quorum of ten, for prayer.
2. Noun: a mediocre thinker who pretends to be a great intellect.

> "Life is like a bed of rusty nails," said the *batlan.*
> "Why is life like a bed of rusty nails?" asked his friend.
> "So who's the philosopher?" replied the *batlan.*

BEHAMA   See *behayma.*

BEHAYMA

Also *behama, beheyme,* and *buhayma.* Pronounced "bah-HAY-meh." From the Hebrew *behemah,* "domesticated animal."

BEHAYMA

1. Noun: a farm animal, particularly a cow.
2. Noun: a dummy.

> There's a Yiddish proverb, "A child at twenty is a *behayma* at twenty-one."

BEHEYME See *behayma*.

BESTITT
Pronounced "beh-STIT." From the German.
Noun: shit, both literally and figuratively.

> "You!" Esther screamed. "Now I'm gonna give yuh-rotten liddle *bestitt*! It's your fault!" (Henry Roth, *Call It Sleep*).

BEYTSEMER See *baitsim*.

BEYTSIM See *baitsim*.

BIALY
Pronounced "bee-AL-lee." From Bialystok, Poland, where the *bialy* was invented.
Noun: a soft, flat baked roll, often topped with onion flakes, that has at its center not a hole, like a *bagel*, but only a depression.

BILLIK

Pronounced "BIL-lick." From the German *billig*, "cheap" or "inexpensive."
Adjective: cheap.

There's a common expression, "as *billik* as borsht."

BLINTZ

From the Ukrainian word for pancake by way of the Yiddish *blintzeh*, "pancake."
Noun: a pancake wrapped around a cheese or fruit filling.

There's a Yiddish curse: "May you turn into a *blintz* and may he turn into a cat and may he eat you up and choke to death on you, so that we will be rid of both of you."

The swift strike of the Israeli army in June 1967 was called a *blintzkrieg* by many journalists.

BLINTZKRIEG   See *blintz.*

BOBBE-MYSEH

Also *bobbeh meisseh* and *boobe-myseh*. Pronounced "BUB-buh-my-suh." From the Yiddish *bubee*, "grandmother," and the Hebrew *mayse*, "tale."
Noun: an old wives' tale.

BOBBEH MEISSEH   See *bobbe-myseh.*

BOBELEH   See *bubehleh.*

BOBKES   See *bubkes.*

BOICHICK   See *boychik.*

BOITSHICK   See *boychik.*

BONDITT

Also *bandit* and *banditt*. Pronounced "bon-DIT." From the German *Bandit*, "bandit."
1. Noun: a beguiler.
2. Noun: a sharpie.

"This *bonditt?* He doesn't even have to open a book—'A' in everything. Albert Einstein the second!" (Philip Roth, *Portnoy's Complaint*).

BOOBE-MYSEH   See *bobbe-myseh.*

BOO-BOO
Also *bubu.* From the Polish *bulba,* "potato." *The Oxford English Dictionary,* however, says *boo-boo* comes from *boob.*
Noun: a minor gaffe; a blooper.

BOPKES   See *bubkes.*

BORAX
Pronounced like the detergent. From the German *borgen,* "to purchase on credit."
(Furniture-store slang) noun: low-quality merchandise; goods that are attractive but shoddy.

BORAX-HOUSE
From the Yiddish *borax,* "cheap goods."
(Furniture-store slang) noun: a store.

BORSHT BELT
The large group of Jewish resorts, including Grossinger's, in the Catskill Mountains in New York State.

BOUBA   See *bubehleh.*

BOUBALA   See *bubehleh.*

BOUBIE   See *bubehleh.*

BOYCHICK   See *boychik.*

BOYCHIK
Also *boichick, boitshick, boychick, boychikel,* and *boytchick.* Pronounced "BOY-chick" and "BOY-chick-el."
Noun: a little boy.

"One time father told him, '*Boichick,* if I'm an exploiter then what are you, since you eat and drink from my exploiting?'" (Wallace Markfield, *To an Early Grave*).

On David Frye's record *Richard Nixon Superstar,* Henry Kissinger says to Billy Graham, "Speaking of economizing, those are pretty nice threads you've got on there, *boychik.*"

"I must confess, in all conscience, that I never heard of the *boychick* in question until I read of his achievement in *The New York Post* the day afterward" (S. J. Perelman, "Walk the Plank, Pussycat —You're on Camera").

"Now the feathers were cooperating beautifully, the bicycle was well behaved, the customers were already calling me by my first name instead of: 'Hey, *boytchick*!' and when Mr. Resnik sent me into the ice-box for the shoulder of lamb, I didn't come back with a shoulder of veal" (Yuri Suhl, "Saved by the Sale").

BOYCHIKEL   See *boychik.*

BOYTCHICK   See *boychik.*

BRAWKHA   See *broche.*

BREN
Pronounced "brehn." Related to the German *brennen,* "to burn."
1. Noun: a real go-getter; a fireball.
2. Noun: someone who thinks fast on his feet. A person who cleverly extricates himself from tight spots.

Here is a story about a *bren:* A Jewish psychoanalyst and an Arab sheikh found themselves sitting next to each other on a commercial flight. The son of Islam decided to get a little shut-eye. Soon the plane encountered turbulence, and the son of Abraham threw up all over the sleeping sheikh. When he woke up, the analyst turned to him and inquired solicitously, "Feeling better now?"

BRISS
From the Hebrew *b'rit,* "covenant."
Noun: the circumcision rite.

In a famous episode of the *Tonight* show, the actor Ed Ames was demonstrating how to throw a tomahawk. He hurled the hatchet at the scalp of a fake man, but it ended up in the target's crotch. Johnny Carson declared, "Welcome to frontier *briss.*"

BROCHE

Also *brawkha, brocheh, brokhe,* and *brucha.* Pronounced "BRAW-kheh."
From the Hebrew *b'rakhah,* "benediction."
Noun: a blessing.

In *Fourth Street East* Jerome Weidman describes a Halloween scene: "The wagon did not stop at the synagogue, although the Indians stopped the war whoops long enough to shout a *brucha,* because they were being hard-pressed by a group of mounted hussars, with shakos topped by ostrich plumes, who had come prancing into Fourth Street behind the Indians."

BROCHEH   See *broche.*

BROKHE   See *broche.*

BRUCHA   See *broche.*

BRUST

Pronounced "broost." Related to the German *Brust,* "breast."
Noun: a breast.

The Pope was dying of a horrible disease. His doctor held out only one ray of hope. "I'm afraid, Your Holiness, that the only possibility of a cure is for you to sleep with a woman."

The Supreme Pontiff was disconsolate, but the doctor was adamant. After intense introspection, the Holy Father concluded that his survival was essential to the well-being of the Church. "I'll go along with your prescription," said the spiritual leader of millions, "but for the sake of security, please find me a woman within the Church—and no one must hear about this."

"Fine," said the doctor. "I'll make all the necessary arrangements."

"Wait," said His Holiness. "I'm really very nervous about people finding out. Can you make sure the woman is blind?"

"That shouldn't be too difficult," replied the doctor as he started out the door.

"Wait!" shouted the Pontiff. "We can't take any chances. She should be deaf, too."

"This may be a little difficult," said the doctor, "but I'll see what I can do." And he left the room.

"Come back!" shouted the infallible embodiment of the Church. "We must be absolutely certain she doesn't talk. Please find me a woman who is dumb as well."

"OK," sighed the doctor, "this will take a miracle but I'm sure God will provide."

The doctor left and was halfway down the hall when the Pope called him back yet again. "One last request," he gasped. "Can you find me one with really big *brusts*?"

B'SULEH

Pronounced "b-SU-leh." From the Hebrew *betulah*, "virgin."
Noun: virgin; young lady.

B'SULIM

Pronounced "b-SU-lim." From the Hebrew.
Noun: hymen.

BUBE   See *bubehleh*.

BUBEE   See *bubehleh*.

BUBELE   See *bubehleh*.

BUBEHLEH

Also *bobeleh, bouba, boubala, boubie, bube, bubee,* and *bubele.*
Pronounced "BOO-buh" or "BOO-buh-lah."
1. Noun: a grandmother.

> "My *bubehleh* ate calf's brain and other delicacies from the old country."

> "Solomon was used to being called a heathen by the *bube*" (Israel Zangwill, *Children of the Ghetto,* 1892).

"If the *bubehleh* had whiskers, she'd be grandpa" and "If the *bubehleh* had wheels, she'd be a trolley car" are Yiddish sayings that mean the same as the English witticism "If wishes were horses, beggars would ride."

BUBKES

Also *bobkes* and *bupkes*. Pronounced "BUB-kiss" or "BUP-kiss." From the Russian *bupkes*, "beans."
Noun: nothing.

When Lauren Bacall and Elizabeth Taylor were both starring on Broadway, they ran into each other at a party at Sardi's. Bacall congratulated Taylor on the success of her show. Taylor introduced her to the man she was with, her bodyguard. Said Bacall to the press: "Liz gets a bodyguard and I get *bubkes*."

"In Chicago we enjoyed the luxurious resources of over a half-million dollars in money and paid attorney time. Our friends in New York got *bubkes*" (in a letter to *The Village Voice*, August 19–25, 1981).

"If the children don't eat their vegetables, they'll get *bubkes* for dessert."

BUBU   See *boo-boo*.

BUHAYMA   See *behayma*.

BULBA   See *bulbe*.

BULBE

Also *bulba*. Pronounced "BULL-bah." From the Polish *bulba*, "potato."
1. Noun: a potato.
2. Noun: a mistake, goof, or screw-up.

BULBENIK

Pronounced "BULL-bah-nick." From the Yiddish *bulbe*, "mistake."
Noun: someone who frequently screws up; a bumbler.

BULVAN

BULVAN
Also *bulvon*. Pronounced "bool-VEN." From the Slavic word for "oaf."
Noun: a big bruiser, lout, or dolt.

BULVON   See *bulvan*.

BUMMERKEH
Pronounced "BOOM-er-kuh." From the German *Bummler*, "idler" or
"loafer."
Noun: a woman bum.

BUPKES   See *bubkes*

BURTCHEN   See *burtshen*.

BURTSHEN
Also *burtchen*. Pronounced "BOORT-chin." From the Slavic.
Verb: to mutter; to grumble.

CHAIM

Also *cheiim*. Pronounced "KHIGH-um." From the Hebrew *chaim*, "life." Noun: life.

The word figures in the common toast *l'Chaim*, "to life."

CHALERYE   See *choleria*.

CHATCHKA

Also *tchotchke, tsatska,* and *tsatske*. Pronounced "CHATCH-kuh." From the Slavic.

1. Noun: a knickknack or trinket.

"Everything's for sale in San Francisco on the street: not just drugs, but puppies, lamps, giant squashes; so many *chatchkas,* so little time" (Richard Goldstein, "Notes on Camping," *The Village Voice,* September 2–8, 1981).

"Some civil liberties fanatics objected on First Amendment grounds to my plan to rid the city of stores with names like 'Tschotchkes 'n' Things' through an ordinance that called for any shopkeeper who failed to spell out a conjunction to be put in the stocks" (Calvin Trillin, *The Nation,* June 24, 1978).

"Reflecting [Goldie] Hawn's heritage as well as her own distinctive predilections, the living-room decor is a mix of oddball stuffed animals and sentimental *tchotchkes* dominated by Early American Folk art and primitive paintings" ("The Secret Life of Goldie Hawn," *Rolling Stone,* March 5, 1981).

2. Noun: a minor cut, scrape, or bruise.
3. Noun (*chatckala* or *tsatskala*): darling; dear; sweetie.
4. Noun: a woman who's a "dish"; a *Playboy* bunny.

CHATCKALA   See *chatchka*.

CHAZEREI   See *chazzerei*.

CHAZERISHE   See *chazzerei*.

CHAZZER

Also *chozzer, khav'r,* and *khazer.* Pronounced "KHAH-zer." From the Hebrew *hazir,* "pig."
Noun: a pig, both literally and figuratively.

> The *chazzer* is the subject of many Yiddish sayings. "If you want to eat *chazzer,* make sure it's good and fat." "If you offer a chair to a *chazzer,* he'll climb on the table." "If you want to become rich, you must sign up for twenty years as a *chazzer.*"

CHAZZEREI

Also *chazerei* and *chozzerai.* Pronounced "khah-zer-EYE." From the Yiddish *chazzer,* "pig."
1. Noun: pig feed.
2. Noun: junk.
3. Adjective (*chazerishe*): unpalatable.

> " 'Mark, what is this *chazerishe* delicacy?' Mrs. Stone probed gingerly with her fork the new dish before her, something sinisterly noncommittal beneath almonds and jujubes" (Leslie Fiedler, *The Second Stone*).

CHEDER

Also *cheyder, heder,* and *kheder.* Pronounced "KHAY-der." From the Hebrew *heder,* "room." The first Hebrew schools, like the first public schools in America, had only one room; thus the derivation of *cheder.*
Noun: Hebrew school.

> "Listen, you think I was just graduated barber college? I was cutting hair when you were a kid in *cheder*!" (S. J. Perelman, *Eastward Ha!*).

CHEIIM   See *chaim*.

CHELM

Pronounced "khelm."
Noun: a mythical city inhabited by lovable morons.

Shlomo had often heard his parents make fun of the people of Chelm. He decided to go to the city to see for himself if they lived up to their stupid reputation. He asked the first resident he met, "What is furry, made of leather, and has five fingers?"

The Chelmnik was completely baffled. He thought long and hard but nothing came to him. "That's a new one on me. What's the answer?"

"A glove," Shlomo revealed.

"That's too tough," complained the Chelmnik. "Ask me an easy question."

"OK," Shlomo replied. "What is furry, made of leather, and has ten fingers?"

The Chelmnik gave a loud whistle. "That's a good one. I give up."

"Well, it's two gloves," Shlomo said.

"Much too hard," said the Chelmnik. "Ask me something really simple."

"All right," said Shlomo. "Who are the Chosen People?"

The Chelmnik's face lit up. "Three gloves!" he shouted.

CHEVRA

Also *khevre*. Pronounced "KHEV-ruh." From the Hebrew *chevrah*, "group of comrades."
Noun: a gang.

CHEYDER   See *cheder.*

CHIMOZZLE   See *schlimazel.*

CHLOPPEH

Pronounced "KHLOP-pah." From the Russian.
Verb: to rain cats and dogs.

CHMALLYEH

Pronounced "KHMOLL-yah." From the Slavic.
Noun: a karate chop.

CHOLERIA

Also *chalerye, kholeria,* and *kholeriye.* Pronounced "khah-LAIR-ee-uh."
From the Hebrew.
1. Noun: cholera; plague.

> *Choleria* figures in many Yiddish curses, such as "May a *choleria*
> consume you" and "May you own a thousand houses that each have
> a thousand rooms with a thousand beds to a room, and may you
> toss from bed to bed with the *choleria*."

> Disease has infected many Yiddishisms: "May they write pre-
> scriptions for him." "A boil is no problem—under the other guy's
> armpit." "May he be beyond the help of any doctor." "May his
> illness plague his mother's milk." "May he be sick and remember."
> "May he have stabbing pains on all sides." "May he own ten
> shipments of gold and spend it all on doctors."

2. Noun: a fishwife; an unpleasant, selfish shrew.

> "Shlomo," said the doctor, "you have four hours to live. Have
> some fun."
> Shlomo rushed home to break the news to his wife. They went
> straight to bed. They made tumultuous love, and then they rolled
> over and went to sleep.
> Two hours later Shlomo woke up and nudged his wife. "Let's
> do it again," he whispered persuasively. "Time is running short."
> His wife agreed, and so they did.
> Afterward they went back to sleep. Half an hour later Shlomo
> woke up his wife. "Let's make love one more time. I have only
> thirty minutes left to live."
> "Don't be so selfish," replied the *choleria*. "Some people have to
> get up and go to work tomorrow."

3. Idiom: "Don't have a nervous *choleria*" means "Don't get hysterical."

CHOZZER   See *chazzer.*

CHOZZERAI   See *chazzerai.*

CHUTSPA   See *chutzpa.*

CHUTSPAH   See *chutzpa*.

CHUTZPA

Also *chutspa, chutspah, chutzpah, hutzpa,* and *khutspe*. Pronounced "KHUTS-puh." From the Hebrew *hutzpah,* "impudence."
Noun: gall; nerve.

"The definition of the Yiddish word *chutzpa,* meaning outrageous gall, is given best in the anecdote of the man who, having killed his parents, throws himself on the mercy of the court as an orphan. If there is a political version of that, it has to be a President who, after submitting a budget with a deficit of about $180 billion, asks for a constitutional amendment to require balanced budgets. Ronald Reagan may not know how to pronounce it, but he is the living embodiment of *chutzpa*" (Richard Cohen, "Chutzpa," *The Washington Post,* May 8, 1982).

"Dear Ann Landers: You have used the word *chutzpah* in your column for the third time since I have been reading you. . . . Please tell me what it means and where it came from" (Ann Landers, March 22, 1982).

"Cafe *Chutzpah:* Brooklyn's own 'Catch a Rising Star and Improvisations,' featuring famous and not yet famous Jewish talents" (a classified ad in *The Village Voice*).

David Frye's Richard Nixon says, "I have been told that I have a lot of *shutspoor*" (from the record *I Am the President*).

" 'He has *hutzpa,*' says [conductor Artur] Rodzinski [of Leonard Bernstein] and illustrates what he means with the story of how Bernstein, a mere thirty-five, dared conduct Beethoven's sacrosanct Ninth Symphony with the great Santa Cecilia chorus in Rome. 'And he had the nerve to move his hips in time to the music. Hutzpa!' " (*Time,* February 4, 1957).

On National Public Radio Alfred A. Knopf said, "When I started out, I was full of *chutzpa*. . . ." (September 18, 1982).

CHUTZPAH   See *chutzpa*.

D

DAVEN

Pronounced "DAH-ven." Origin unknown.
Verb: to pray.

DIBIK   See *dybbuk.*

DONSTAIRSIKEH

Pronounced "don-STAIR-zi-kuh."
Noun: the downstairs neighbor.

DOPPES

Pronounced "DOP-piss."
Noun: a bystander who offers help not with actions but with words.

DRAIKOPF

DRAIKOPF

Also *draykop, draykopf,* and *draykup.* Pronounced "DRAY-kawp." From
the German *drayen,* "to turn," and *Kopf,* "head." Literally, a "turn-head."

1. Noun: a sophist; someone who turns facts to his own advantage.
2. Noun: someone whose head is turned around; a person who is confused.

DRAYKOP   See *draikopf.*

DRAYKOPF   See *draikopf.*

DRAYKUP   See *draikopf.*

DRECK

Also *drek.* From the German *Dreck,* "dung."
1. Noun: shit—both literally and figuratively.

> "I don't say the *goyim* don't give you *dreck,* but their *dreck* has at least a *finesse,*" said Mr. Herberg (Wallace Markfield, *Teitlebaum's Window*).

2. Exclamation: Drat! Shit!
3. Adjective (*dreckische*): shitty.

> "He laughed with his bare breath. 'Well, I think we'll leave your *dreckische* pants out here. Phew!'" (Saul Bellow, *Herzog*).

DRECKISCHE   See *dreck.*

DREDL   See *dreydel.*

DREK   See *dreck.*

DREYDEL

Also *dredl.* Pronounced "DRAY-dull." From the German *drayen,* "to turn."
Noun: a little four-sided top that Jewish kids play with on Chanukah. Each side has a Hebrew letter written on it. The letter the top lands on determines what goodies the child gets.

DYBBUK

Also *dibik.* Pronounced "DIB-book." From the Hebrew "to cling."
1. Noun: the ghost of a dead person that takes possession of a living person who had wronged him or her when alive.
2. Noun: an evil spirit; an incubus.

DYBBUK

"We'll take a few more X rays to be absolutely positive, but the way I see it, my friend, it's definitely a *dybbuk*" (Wallace Markfield, *Teitlebaum's Window*).

"Such things are forbidden on the Sabbath, but I had forgotten my religion: surely there was a *dybbuk* in me" (Isaac Bashevis Singer, "Fire").

"She asked me why the clock was running backward, and I told her to pay more attention to her cereal-eating; my alternative being to admit to her that the only explanation that I had been able to think of was that our clock had been invaded by a *dybbuk*, a bloody-minded cousin of the *dybbuk* in our washing machine" (Calvin Trillin, *The Nation*, February 2, 1980).

DZHLOB   See *zhlub*.

ECHT

Pronounced "echt." From the German *echt,* "authentic."
Adjective: genuine.

> "I wanted to go there because I had never before tried authentic, that is to say *echt,* Jewish cuisine and also because—well, when in Flatbush . . ." (William Styron, *Sophie's Choice*).

EINREDENISH

Pronounced "INE-red-en-ish." Related to the German *einreden,* "to persuade."
Noun: a self-induced delusion.

EIZEL

Pronounced "EYE-zel." From the German *Esel,* "donkey" or "fool."
Noun: a fool.

EMES

Pronounced "EHM-ess."
Exclamation: Honest! Truly!

EPIS See *eppis.*

EPPES See *eppis.*

EPPIS

Also *epis* and *eppes.* Pronounced "EH-piss." From the German.
1. Noun: something.

> The phrase "Make something of it" is a translation of a Yiddish expression involving *eppis.*

2. Interjection: "God knows why!"

"Instead of money, *real* money with which you can buy whatever you like, I got *epis* a green little book in a yellow envelope and—that's all!" (Moishe Nadir, "My First Deposit," translated by Nathan Ausubel).

ESSEN

Pronounced "ES-sen." From the German *essen*, "to eat."
Verb: to eat.

FAIGELEH

Also *faygala* and *faygeleh*. Pronounced "FAY-guh-luh." From the German *Vogel*, "bird."
1. Noun: a little bird.
2. Noun: a homosexual.

> "Not so fast," objected the old man. "I got a couple of dead *faygelehs* I want to watch on television tonight" (Joseph Heller, *Good As Gold*).

FARANTVORTLECH

Pronounced "FAR-ant-vort-lech." From the German *verantwortlich*, "responsible."
Adjective: responsible; accountable.

FARBISSENEH

Pronounced "far-BISS-e-neh." From the German *verbissen*, "grim" or "morose."
Noun or adjective (*farbissener* for a man): a bitter woman.

> "Muriel had always been embittered and self-centered—the *farbisseneh* one, his mother would say, an objection made more in woe than reprimand" (Joseph Heller, *Good As Gold*).

FARBISSENER See *farbisseneh*.

FARBLONDJHET

Also *farblondzhet*. Pronounced "fer-BLAWN-jet." From the Slavic *blondzhen*, "to wander blindly."
Adjective: wandering about aimlessly; confused.

Alexander Haig was *farblondjhet* when he declared, "I'm in charge here now."

FARBLONDZHET   See *farblondjhet*.

FARMATERT
Pronounced "far-MA-turt." From the German *matt*, "exhausted."
Adjective: utterly tired.

FARMISHT
Pronounced "far-MISHT." From the German *vermischen*, "to mix."
Adjective: mixed up; confused emotionally.

FARPOTSHKET
Pronounced "far-POTSH-ket." From the German *Patsche*, "difficulty" or "mess."
Adjective: messed up.

FARPUTZT

FARPUTZT
Pronounced "far-PUTST." From the German *putzen*, "to dress."
Adjective: decked out.

FARSHTINKENER
Also *farshtunkener*. Pronounced "fer-SHTINK-e-neh." From the German *verstinken*, "to stink up."
Adjective: stinking.

"And when Sophie again affirmed all that she had been saying, he looked at her with compassion and murmured, very bitterly for him, 'Oy vey, what a *farshtinkener* world is this' " (William Styron, *Sophie's Choice*).

FARSHTUNKENER   See *farshtinkener.*

FARSHVITST
Pronounced "far-SHVITST." From the German *schwitzen,* "to sweat." Adjective: sweaty.

In *The Taste of Yiddish* Lillian Mermin Feinsilver reports hearing a radio announcer on WNBC say, "If you've just lugged the groceries and are all *farshvitst,* try cooling off with some Tetley Tea."

FARTOOTST
Pronounced "far-TOOT-st." From the German *verdutzen,* "to be bewildered."
Adjective: mixed up.

The Reverend Billy Graham was *fartootst* when, after his trip to the Soviet Union in the spring of 1982, he said: "I noticed no religious persecution."

FARTUMELT
Pronounced "far-TOO-melt." From the German *tummeln,* "to romp about" or "to scuffle."
Adjective: disoriented; confused.

FAYGALA   See *faigeleh.*

FAYGELEH   See *faigeleh.*

FEH
Pronounced like the "fe" in "fetter."
Exclamation: Ugh! Phooey! Baloney!

FEINSCHMECKER

Pronounced "FINE-shmeck-er." From the German *fein,* "cultivated,"
and *schmecken,* "to taste." Literally, a "cultivated taster."
Noun: someone who has a discerning palate; a gourmand.

> In *Eastward Ha!* S. J. Perelman has Valéry Giscard d'Estaing, the
> former president of France, say: "Is all in readiness, then, to welcome
> back that acclaimed boulevardier, *Feinschmecker,* and Yankee globe-
> trotter, which he is without peer in this century if one overlooks
> Wilfred Thesiger, Henri de Monfried and Freya Stark?"

FONFER   See *fonfeven.*

FONFEVEN

Pronounced "FON-fev-en." From the Slavic "to talk through the nose."
1. Verb: to nasalize.
2. Verb: to double-talk.
3. Noun (*fonfer*): a double-talker; a swindler.

FRESSEN

Pronounced "FRESS-en." From the German *fressen,* "to eat." This German verb is normally reserved for animals; the verb *essen,* "to eat," is used
for people.
Verb: to gobble; to eat food the way an animal does.
2. Noun. (*fresser*): a gobbler.

> "It's Pac-Man, the a-maze-ing video game! Yes, this fabulous
> *fresser* is gleefully gobbling his way across America!" (Jews for
> Jesus, "Pac-Man Fever").

FRIM

Also *frum.* Pronounced "frum." From the German *fromm,* "pious."
Adjective: devout.

> "On Saturdays, Jews who were *frim* . . . would no more think
> of moving about in any form of vehicular transportation than they
> would think of striking a match or even a wife" (Jerome Weidman,
> *Last Respects*).

FROSK

Pronounced "frahsk."
Verb: to smack hard.

"If you get fresh with her, she'll *frosk* you."

FRUM   See *frim*.

FUTZ
SHTUP
PUTZ
YENTZEN

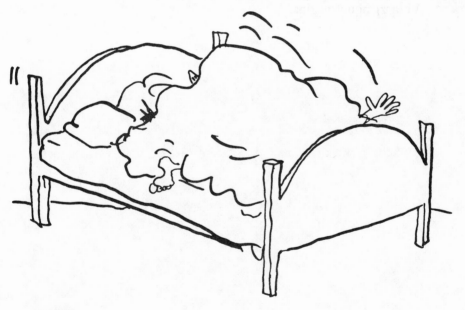

FUTZ

Pronounced "futs."
1. Verb: to copulate.
2. Verb ("to *futz* around"): to screw around. Yiddish slang words for
"fornicate," like the English *fuck* and *screw,* also mean "to play around."

"But I also love rain. Real, pouring rain, not the drizzling kind. If it's going to rain, then rain! Don't just *futz* around" (Lana Turner, *Lana: The Lady, the Legend, the Truth*).

God and His son were playing golf. On the first hole Jesus got off a perfect shot that arced beautifully and went straight down into the hole. God also had a tremendous shot, but just before the ball went into the hole, an eagle swooped down out of the sky, snatched the ball, and flew off into the forest. Moments later a squirrel ran out of the forest with a golf ball in its mouth. The squirrel darted around aimlessly on the green. Soon a large bear emerged from the forest and chased the squirrel over to the hole, into which it dropped the ball. Jesus turned to his Dad: "Are you going to play golf or are you going to *futz* around?"

3. Adjective (*futzed* up): fucked up, as in having consumed too many illegal, mind-expanding substances, i.e., drugs.
4. (Vulgar) noun: vagina.

G

GANEF See *gonif.*

GANEV See *gonif.*

GANIF See *gonif.*

GAON

GAON
Pronounced "GUY-own." From the Hebrew.
Noun: a genius.

> "*Gevalt!* I'm going to give birth to a *gaon.* I've a *tzaddik* ['wise man'] in my belly!" (Isaac Meier Dick, "Two Strangers Came to Town," translated by Nathan Ausubel).

GEFERLECH
Pronounced "ge-FAIR-lich." From the German *gefährlich,* "dangerous."
Adjective: terrible.
> Used as in "It's not *geferlech*" ("It's nothing to worry about").

GEHAKTEH TSORES
Pronounced "ge-HAHK-tah-TSOR-es." From the Yiddish *hok,* "chop," and *tsores,* "troubles." Literally, "chopped-up troubles."
Noun: total misery.

There's a Yiddish expression, *"Gehakteh leber* ['chopped liver'] is better than *gehakteh tsores."*

"BETTER TO BE WITH A WISE MAN IN GEHENNA . . .

. . . THAN WITH A FOOL IN PARADISE"

GEHENNA

Pronounced "gay-HEN-nuh." From the Hebrew *Gehinom.*
Noun: hell.

Strictly speaking, there is no hell in Judaism. But south of Jerusalem lay the Valley of Gehinom, where pagans sacrificed infants to the god Moloch and practiced other unmentionably disgusting rites.

Some Yiddish proverbs: "Better to be with a wise man in *Gehenna* than with a fool in paradise" and *"Gehenna* is not as bad as the road to it."

GELIBTEH

Pronounced "gel-IB-teh." From the German *Geliebte,* "beloved."
Noun: a beloved woman. (A beloved man is a *gelibter.*)

GELT

From the German *Geld,* "money."
Noun: money.

Two Yiddish proverbs: "Lost years are worse than lost *gelt"* and "The world is held up by three things: *gelt, gelt,* and *gelt."*

In the May 19, 1979, issue of *The Nation,* Calvin Trillin reports that when he worked in the research department of Time Inc., he was once asked to find the name of the longest street in London that was uninterrupted by intersections. "For a while," Trillin wrote, "I tried to imagine the sentence of a *Fortune* story such a fact might fit into ('Sophisticated Londoners have always known, in the way they know that the longest street uninterrupted by intersections is Something Street, that the most powerful figure in the Bank of England is the daft but wily Lord Boode of *Gelt'*)."

GENUG
Pronounced "geh-NOOG." From the German *genug,* "enough."
Exclamation: Enough!

GESCHEFT   See *gesheft.*

GESHEFT
Also *gescheft.*
Pronounced "ge-SHEFT." From the German *Geschäft,* "business."
Noun: business.

A typical Yiddish curse: "May he own a large *gesheft* and may he never have in stock what is asked for and may he only have in stock what is never asked for."

The Yiddish idiom "the whole *gesheft*" means the same as the English idiom "the whole business." Example: "What a piece of work is a man, and the firmament fretted with gold—but the whole *gescheft* bores him" (Saul Bellow, *The Adventures of Augie March*).

GESHMAK
Pronounced "ge-SHMAHCK." From the German *Geshmack,* "taste" or "flavor."
Adjective: delicious; yummy.

GESHREI
Pronounced "ge-SHRY." From the German *Geschrei,* "shriek" or "outcry."
Noun: a scream, clamor, or yell.

"At that point, the self-flagellationists of the West—who cannot abide the thought of a clear-cut victory by a democratic power in the Falklands or in Lebanon—will let loose a tremendous *geshrei*" (William Safire, "The Liberation of Lebanon," *The New York Times,* June 11, 1982).

GESHTANK

Pronounced "ge-SHTOONK." Related to the German *stinken,* "to stink."
Adjective: foul-smelling.

GESHVOLLEN

Pronounced "geh-SHVOLL-en." From the German *geschwollen,* "swollen."
Adjective: swollen pride.

A Yiddish adage that captures the *geshvollen* personality is: "They're in love—he with himself and she with herself."

GEVALT

Pronounced "geh-VAULT." From the German *Gewalt,* "power," "authority," or "force."
Exclamation: Help! Oh my God!

There's the Yiddish saying "When a Jew hits you, he cries *'Gevalt!'* "

GLITCH

Pronounced "glitch." From the Yiddish *glitschen,* "to slip or skid."
1. Noun: a sudden surge of power, or other technological irregularity, that interferes with the smooth operation of a computer.
2. Noun: a systemic defect; a fly in the ointment.

"Weinberger said that if the Israelis had any protest, it should have been directed immediately to the leaders of the international military force at the port. He played down the blockade, however, calling it a 'little *glitch*' " (*The Boston Globe,* August 24, 1982).

3. Verb: to do something inadvertently that cuts short the execution of a computer program.
4. (Particle-physics patois) noun: an unexpected irregularity in a data run.

GLITZ

Pronounced "glitz." From the German *Glitzer*, "glitter."
1. Noun: glitter.
2. Adjective (*glitzy*): showy; ostentatious; gaudy.

Glitzy, as word *maven* William Safire correctly noted, is Yinglish rather than a portmanteau of *glitter* and *ritzy*.

GLITZY   See *glitz*.

GOLEM

Also *goylem*. Pronounced "GO-lum." From the Hebrew *golem*, "dummy."
Noun: a robot; a lifeless but lifelike creation (such as Frankenstein); a clay figure that cannot speak.

In the sixteenth century Rabbi Judah Loew of Prague brought a *golem* to life by putting in its mouth a piece of paper on which was spelled God's special, secret name. The *golem* helped the rabbi combat anti-Semitism. It became increasingly human, however, and the rabbi had to destroy it before he·lost control of it.

" 'What do you think of that Nathan? Don't he break your balls?' A sudden light glowed in his lusterless eyes, his voice becoming conspiratorial. 'You know what I think he is? A *golem*, that's what. Some kind of a golem!' " (William Styron, *Sophie's Choice*).

"What a belief that the great masses are pails into which you can pour any kind of slop . . . and make them act like your *golem*!" (R. Berenson, *One Year's Reading*).

GONIF

Also *ganef, ganev, ganif, goniff, gonoph, gonov, gunif,* and *gunnif.* Pronounced "GONE-if." From the Hebrew *ganav*, "thief."
1. Noun: a crook.

"He's as obstinate a young *gonoph* as I know. He WON'T move on" (Charles Dickens, *Bleak House*, 1853). *The Oxford English Dictionary* notes that this is the first time *gonif* was used in written English.

GONIF

" 'There's a thief in the house!' the rabbi shouted, 'There's a *ganef*!' Rabbi Leonard W. Stern dutifully scanned the faces of the 30 hospital patients for the culprit, the one who made off with the matzoh. . . ." (*The New York Times,* April 17, 1981).

2. Noun: someone who is clever, perhaps to the point of being diabolical.
3. Noun: a swindler.

"Besides, I question the collective term 'pack' that you employ. While eminently proper for hounds or wolves, would it not be more accurate to describe yourselves as a *goniff* of swindlers?" (S. J. Perelman, "One Order of Blintzes, and Hold the Flimflam").

"The Riggs–King match was held in September, 1973. I never wrote about it afterward—partly because I didn't want to repeat myself and partly because I had mixed feelings about the outcome. I knew that it was a triumph for women's tennis, and it was even a small triumph for the women journalists at it—we won $800 from Riggs. But when the circus was over, I felt sorry for Riggs. I thought he was a harmless *goniff,* and I was sad that his fifteen minutes were up—it had been fun" (Nora Ephron, "The Pig," *Crazy Salad*).

4. Noun: a precocious child.

GONIFF   See *gonif*.

GONOPH   See *gonif*.

GONOV   See *gonif*.

GORNISHT
Pronounced "GAWR-nisht."
Noun: nothing.

A man who was being chased by a vicious vampire turned around and whipped out a cross. The vampire said, " *'svet gornisht helfen"* ("nothing will help").

GOT   See *Gott*.

GOTT
Also *Got*. Pronounced "gawt."
Noun: God.

Many Yiddish proverbs involve *Gott*. "If *Gott* willed it, a broom could shoot." "If *Gott* lived on earth, all his windows would be broken." "He owes *Gott* for his soul and the butcher for his meat."

Menachem Begin was visiting Ronald Reagan in the White House. "Why do you have three phones?" Begin asked, pointing to a red one, a blue one, and a white one on Reagan's desk.

"Oh," the President replied, "the red phone is a hotline to the Kremlin, the white phone is a hotline to the capitals of my fifty states and the blue one is a hotline to God."

"You have a hotline to *Gott*?" gasped Begin in amazement. "Do you mind if I use it? I have a few things to ask Him."

"Go right ahead," Reagan replied.

Begin talked to God for ten minutes or so. When he got off the phone, he asked Reagan how much that would be.

"Normally," the President said, "I wouldn't charge you anything. But since I'm having such difficulties balancing the budget, I'll charge you at cost—three thousand dollars." Begin gave him the money.

Six months later Reagan was visiting Begin in Israel and noticed three phones—a red one, a white one, and a blue one—on the Prime Minister's desk. "What are these for?" asked Reagan.

"*Nu,*" Begin replied, "the red phone is a hotline to Cairo, the white one is a hotline to my borders, and the blue phone is a hotline to *Gott.*"

"Do you mind if I speak to him?" Reagan asked. Begin told him to go right ahead. When the President was finished, he asked Begin how much the call cost.

"Ten cents," Begin said.

"Ten cents?" repeated Reagan. "That can't be. I was on the phone at least five minutes."

"Don't worry," replied Begin. "From here it's a local call."

GOYIM

GOY

Pronounced "goy." From the Hebrew *goy,* "nation." The plural of *goy* is the Yiddish *goyim* or the Yinglish *goys.*
1. Noun: a non-Jew.

" 'I give you my permission to see Gordon.' Then he said, softly, 'But Reuben, do not become a *goy*' " (Chaim Potok, *The Promise*).

"Thank Thee O lord God King of the Universe for not having made me, in addition to being a *goy,* a woman (Leslie Fiedler, *The Second Stone*).

"The Jews I despise for their narrow-mindedness, their self-righteousness, the incredibly bizarre sense that these cave men who are my parents and relatives have somehow gotten of their own superiority—but when it comes to tawdriness and cheapness, to beliefs that would shame even a gorilla, you simply cannot top the *goyim*" (Philip Roth, *Portnoy's Complaint*).

2. Noun: a nonreligious Jew.
3. Noun: someone who is unfeeling and insensitive.
4. Adjective (*goyishe*): gentile.

The Foreword to John Updike's fictitious biography, *Bech: A Book,* is a "letter" from Henry Bech to Updike. Bech wrote, in part, "I'm sure that when with that blithe *goyishe* brass I will never cease to grovel at, you approached me for a 'word or two by way of preface,' you were bargaining for a benediction, not a curse."

The phrase *goyishe mazel* (literally, "gentile luck") means "undeserved fortune." *Goyishe kop* ("gentile head") means "stupidity."

GOYIM   See *goy.*

GOYISHE MAZEL

GOYISHE   See *goy.*

GOYLEM   See *golem.*

GRAUB

Also *grauber, grob,* and *grober.* Pronounced so that the "au" rhymes with "Mao." From the German *grob,* "coarse," "uncouth," or "rude."
1. Adjective (also *grobyungish*): brutish; vulgar.
2. Noun (*graubyon*): a brute.
3. Noun (*grauber yung* or *grober yung*): "coarse young;" a lout.

GRAUBER   See *graub.*

GRAUBYON   See *graub.*

GREPS

Also *grepts.* Pronounced "greptz." From the German.
1. Verb: to belch.
2. Noun: a belch or burp.

      On a Los Angeles radio station Lee Chandler once told a gag about Israel inventing a *greps* bomb.

GREPTS   See *greps.*

GROB   See *graub.*

GROBER   See *graub.*

GROBYUNGISH   See *graub.*

GUNIF   See *gonif.*

GUNIFF   See *gonif.*

HAIMISH

Also *heimisch*. Pronounced "HAY-mish." From the German *Heim*, "home."
Adjective: homey; cozy.

"I feel cheerful, generally. People find fault with it. A drunken lady asked me last week what the hell my problem was. She said I was a compulsive-*heimisch* type" (Saul Bellow, *Humboldt's Gift*).

"His friends are throwing him a party that, according to Mr. Buchwald, the humorist, is going to be 'a real *haimish* evening'" (Barbara Gamarekian, "A Favorite Pharmacist Is the Guest of Honor," *The New York Times*, March 30, 1982).

HAK   See *hok*.

HALEVAI   See *alevay*.

HALEVAY   See *alevay*.

HANDLEN

Pronounced "HOND-len." From the German *Handel*, "bargain."
1. Verb: to do business; to engage in commerce.
2. Verb: to haggle over prices.

Even a rabbi has to *handlen*, as Bruno Lessing's "The Story of Sara" makes clear:
"Are they fresh?"
"They were swimming in the sea this very day, Herr Rabbi. They could not be fresher if they were alive. And the price is—Oh, you will laugh at me when I tell you—only twelve cents a pound."

"Come, come, my good mother, tell me without joking what they cost. This big one, and that little one over there."

"But Herr Rabbi, you surely cannot mean that that is too much. Well, well—an old friend—eleven cents, we'll say."

HEDER   See *cheder.*

HEIMISCH   See *haimish.*

HELDISH
Pronounced "HELD-ish." From the German *Held,* "hero."
Adjective: brave.

HINTEN
Pronounced "HIN-tin." From the German *hinten,* "in the rear."
Noun: buttocks.

A Yiddish curse goes: "May he walk on his hands for as many years as he walked on his feet and whatever years he has left, may he push himself along on his *hinten.*"

HITSKOP
Pronounced "HITS-kawp." From the German *Hitz,* "heat," "fever," or "passion," and the Yiddish *kop,* "head."
Literally, a "hothead."
Noun: someone who is easily excitable.

HOCK   See *hok.*

HOK
Also *hak* and *hock.* Pronounced "hahk." From the German *Hack,* "strike" or "blow."
Verb: to strike, bang, or chop.

An ad in the September 1957 issue of *Commentary* shows a woman struggling to chop up a fish that has a malicious smile. The ad says, "Quit *'hockin'* and messin'. Get Mother's Gefilte Fish, ready to serve."

There's the popular expression "*Hok a tchynik*" ("Bang on the tea kettle"), which means "to yak or nag endlessly." The expression is often heard in the negative: *"Hok mir nisht kain tchynik"* ("Stop yakking").

HOLDUPNIK
Pronounced "hold-UP-nick." See the entry for *-nik*.
Noun: a mugger.

HOTCHA
Pronounced "HAH-cha." This word could be related to the English *hot*.

Nevertheless, in *American Speech*, A. A. Roback suggests that *hotcha* comes from the Yiddish *hotsa*, "hop." It is common, Roback says, for parents to encourage "an infant to dance while shaking it. As it hops up and down, moving its little legs, the parents keep repeating *hotsa*, i.e., 'hop-hop-hop' (in Yiddish)." The child evidently comes to associate *hotsa* with rapid entertainment, such as dancing one might see on the stage, and learns to shout appreciatively at such times.

Exclamation: Great! A cry of approval, uttered especially at lively theatrical events. Sometimes the cry is a sarcastic one.

Groucho Marx was fond of exclaiming *"Hotcha!"*

HUBBA-HUBBA
Pronounced "hubah-hubah." The derivation is uncertain but it may be Yiddish.

The origin of *hubba-hubba* caused a big hubbub in the periodical *American Speech*. In the May 1955 issue Thomas Pyles suggested that the word came from *hibba-hibba*, which he described as a sound of revelry heard at gatherings of Jews. In the December issue of that year, A. A. Roback took issue with this explanation. "I have never heard *hibba-hibba* used as a sound of revelry, joy, or general noise at Jewish parties. . . . It reminds me of the FBI investigator who came to a conclusion that a certain engagement celebration was a Communist meeting because he heard the people merrily shouting 'Molotov' [*mazel tov,* 'good luck']."

Roback, however, goes on to suggest a Yiddish origin: "The habit of tossing a baby up into the air or between the parents is probably not peculiar to young Jewish couples. What is relevant here, however, is that each throw is accompanied by the words *khup* ('catch') *a yingele* for a little boy and *khup a meydele* for a little girl. Most frequently, the object is omitted and the verb alone, i.e., *khup,* together with the article *a* for rhythm, is articulated." Roback assures us that the baby comes to associate the "khuppa-khuppa" with gaiety of any sort. *Hubba-hubba* for this etymological sortie.

Exclamation: Bravo!

An expression of enthusiastic approval, used especially by G.I.'s in World War II in reference to an attractive woman. Also shouted at Broadway shows and similar events.

HUTZPA   See *chutzpa.*

KABTSEN

Also *kabts'n, kabtzen,* and *koptzen.* Pronounced "COP-son." From the Hebrew *kabotz,* "to collect."

1. Noun: a pauper.
2. Noun: a good-for-nothing.

KABTS'N   See *kabtsen.*

KABTZEN   See *kabtsen.*

KADDISH

Pronounced "CAH-dish." From the Aramaic.

Noun: a prayer for the dead.

> " 'I have no son to say *Kaddish* for my soul when I am dead. Will you be my *Kaddish,* Shaya? Will you observe the anniversary of my death?' he queried, in a beseeching tone which the young man had never heard from him" (Abraham Cahan, "The Imported Bridegroom," 1898).

KADOCHES

Also *kadokhes.* Pronounced "kah-DOH-khus." From the Hebrew *kadahat,* "shaking with heat and with cold."

1. Noun: convulsions, malaria, and fever.
2. (Ironic) noun: less than nothing; good-for-nothing.

> Used in the idiomatic phrase *"Er hat kadoches"* (literally, "He has a fever"), which means "He's good-for-nothing." Another example: *"Ikh vel im geben a kadoches"* (literally, "I'll give him a fever"), or "He'll get less than nothing from me."

KADOKHES   See *kadoches.*

KAKAPITSHI

Also *kakepitsi.* Pronounced "KAH-kah-peet-she." From *ka ka,* baby talk for "shit" via German. And also perhaps from *pee,* baby talk for "piss."
1. Noun: an inedible concoction.
2. Noun: a conglomeration.

KAKEPITSI   See *kakapitshi.*

KALAMUTNEH

Pronounced "kal-ah-MUT-neh."
Adjective: gloomy.

> "THE DEAF MAN HEARD A MUTE DESCRIBE
> HOW A BLIND MAN WATCHED A KALIKEH RUN."

KALIKEH

Also *kalyeke, kalyekeh, kolyika,* and *kolyike.*
Pronounced "CAL-ih-keh."
1. Noun: a crippled woman. (A crippled man is a *kalyeker.*)

The Yiddish proverb "The deaf man heard a mute describe how a blind man watched a *kalikeh* run" embodies the same truth as the English phrase "the blind leading the blind."

2. Noun: a misfit.
3. Noun: an inept craftsman or performer.

KALYEKE   See *kalikeh*.

KALYEKEH   See *kalikeh*.

KALYEKER   See *kalikeh*.

KAMTSAN
Pronounced "KAHMT-sahn." From the Hebrew *kamtzan*, "miser."
Noun: a tightwad; a stingy person.

> "I enjoyed the party," Shlomo said to his host. "You're quite a cook. I had five of your little cakes."
> "You ate six," replied the *kamtsan*, "but who's counting?"

KANEH
Pronounced "CON-eh."
Noun: an enema.

KAPORA   See *kapore*.

KAPORE
Also *kapora* and *kaporeh*. Pronounced "ca-POOR-eh." From the Hebrew *kaparah*, "forgiveness."
1. Noun: forgiveness; atonement; sacrifice.

> A traditional ritual, *shlogn kapores* ("beating atonement"), consists of swinging a rooster three times over the head of a repentant sinner so that his sins are transferred to the fowl. The rooster is then slaughtered and presented to the poor.

2. (Slang) noun: a good-for-nothing.

KAPOREH   See *kapore*.

KASHE

Pronounced "CA-shuh." From the Russian *kasha,* "mush cereal."
1. Noun: mush cereal.
2. Noun: a mess; a mix-up.
3. Noun: a question. From the Hebrew *kushyah,* "question." On the first eve of Passover the youngest male child asks *di fir kashes* (the "Four Questions").

KASNIK

Also *keisennik.* Pronounced "CAHZ-nick."
Noun: a hothead; an angry person.

KASOKEH

Also *kosokeh.* Pronounced "KAS-oh-keh."
Adjective: cross-eyed.

KAYN AYNHOREH

Also *kina hora.* Pronounced "kine-ine-HAW-ruh." From the German *kein,* "no," and the Hebrew *ayin hara,* "evil eye."
Exclamation: Spare us the evil eye! Knock on wood!

The evil eye was much feared in traditional Judaism. The Talmud says, "Ninety-nine persons die of an evil eye against one in the natural cause." Perhaps the word *canary* in the slang American English expression "Don't give me the canary" is a barbaric pronunciation of *kayn aynhoreh.*

"Shlomo thinks he had a good interview with the Harvard Admissions Office, *kayn aynhoreh.*"

KEISENNIK See *kasnik.*

KEMFER

Pronounced "KEMF-en." From the German *kampfen,* "to fight."
Noun: a fighter; a militant supporter of a cause.

"Menachem Begin and Yasir Arafat are real *kemfers.*"

KHAV'R See *chazzer.*

KHAZER   See *chazzer.*

KHEDER   See *cheder.*

KHEVRE   See *chevra.*

KHOLERIA   See *choleria.*

KHOLERIYE   See *choleria.*

KHUTSPE   See *chutzpa.*

KIBBITZ

Also *kibitz.* Pronounced "KIB-its." From the German *Kiebitz,* a "peewit" or "lapwing," a bird known for its hovering.

"The eggs of the peewit," wrote Herman Post in the *New York Evening Post* (February 15, 1929), "are very much sought after for their delicious taste. They are laid on the ground. The bird, to protect the eggs, flies frantically around the heads of people looking for them." The German word *Kiebitz* apparently comes from the sound the bird makes.

1. Verb: to comment while others are playing a game; to offer gratuitous advice.
2. Noun (*kibbitzer*): a meddlesome onlooker.

"What I want to tell you may revolt you, but I hope you have more understanding for human weakness than the *kibitzers* in the Café Royal" (Isaac Bashevis Singer, "Advice").

KIBITZ   See *kibbitz.*

KIBITZER   See *kibbitz.*

KIBOSH

Pronounced "KY-bosh." Origin unknown, but perhaps Yiddish.
1. Exclamation: Nonsense! Bosh!
2. Verb ("to put the *kibosh* on"): to make into nonsense; to jinx; to frustrate.

"I was praying that the kid wouldn't come down out of the cab, and put the 'kibosh' on me" (Jack London, *The Road,* 1907).

KIKE

Pronounced "kike." Perhaps from the Yiddish *kaykel*, "circle."

Leo Rosten reports that illiterate Jewish immigrants signed their names on immigration forms not with the customary "X," which had Christian overtones for them, but with a circle. For the same reason, Jewish shopkeepers used circles instead of X's in their account books. This explanation seems too pat, however, because it depends on the immigrant-baiters knowing the Yiddish word for circle. Much more plausible is the theory that *kike* is derived from the "-sky" and "-ski" endings of many Ashkenazic names.
(Vulgar) noun: a Jew.

"He told her, 'Calling you a black woman is as inexact as calling me a pink man.' She responded promptly. 'Calling me a Negress is as insulting as calling you a *kike*'" (John Updike, *Bech: A Book*).

"So that's how I came to pitchin', Angela. I got myself a big pile a' rocks, and I lined up these beer and whiskey bottles that I'd fish outta the bay, and I'd stand about fifty feet away, and then I'd start throwing. You mick bastard! You wop bastard! You *kike* bastard! You nigger bastard! You Hun son of a bitch! That's how I developed my pick-off play" (Philip Roth, *The Great American Novel*).

KINA HORA   See *kayn aynhoreh.*

KISHKA

Also *kishke.* Pronounced "KISH-kuh." From the Russian word for "intestines."
1. Noun: intestine.

"Want a shot in the *kishkas*?" the mother of one of the authors used to say when he did something that got on her nerves.

"When they were on the road again, Hymie said disgustedly, 'It's one damn repair after another.' 'Age is wearing it away,' the old man said. 'Its *kishkes* are rotten like mine'" (Philip Moss, "To the Mountains").

" 'Tip-top New York-style corned beef that melts in the *kishkes*!' trumpeted the menu" (S. J. Perelman, *Eastward Ha!*).

"The smiles took a shot in the *kishke* when they saw me. They gave me the hairy eyeball, then turned the X-ray looks on each other" (Jerome Weidman, *Last Respects*).

2. Noun: stuffed derma.

In 1963 one of the Top 40 hits was "Who Stole the *Kishke*?"

KISHKE   See *kishka*.

KLAPERKEH
Pronounced "KLAP-er-keh."
Noun: a woman who is a chatterbox.

KLIPE   See *klipeh*.

KLIPEH
Also *klipe* and *klippe*. Pronounced "CLIP-eh." From the Hebrew *klipah*, "rind."
1. Noun: a hag, a shrew.
2. Noun: a demonic woman.

KLIPPE   See *klipeh*.

KLOGMUTER
Pronounced "CLOG-moo-ter."
Noun: a complainer or whiner.

Shlomo's mother gave him two ties, a red one and a blue one. He thanked her profusely and immediately put on the red one. "Look, Ma, it's beautiful," Shlomo said.
"What's the matter?," asked the *klogmuter*, "you don't like the blue tie?"

KLOTS-KASHE
Pronounced "CLOTS-CA-shuh." From the German *Klotz*, "wooden beam" or "blockhead," and the Hebrew *kushyah*, "question."

Noun: A simply worded but difficult question artfully interjected into a discussion or presentation that is proceeding smoothly. The purpose of the question is to derail the discussion or to throw off the speaker.

Suppose a rabbi was telling his charges that the Jews are the Chosen People. A child might pipe up with the *klots-kashe* "How can Jews be the Chosen People if the Declaration of Independence affirms that all men are created equal?" And if the stunned rabbi continued with his impassioned address, insisting that Jesus Christ cannot be the son of God because immaculate conception is a biological impossibility, the same child might ask another *klots-kashe:* "If God is omnipotent, why can't He have a child without engaging in intercourse?" (Incidentally, Ozzie Freedman pursues both these questions in Philip Roth's "The Conversion of the Jews.")

A mundane *klots-kashe* would be if someone interrupted the editor-in-chief of *Scientific American* at an editorial meeting to ask, "What is science?"

KLOYMERSHT
Pronounced "CLOY-mairsht." From the Hebrew *k'lomar,* "as if it were." Adjective: pretended.

"John Hinkley was the *kloymersht* boyfriend of Jodie Foster."

KLUG
Pronounced "cloog." From the German *klug,* "clever." Adjective: smart.

"A *klug* man hears one word and understands two" is an old Yiddish proverb.

KLUPPER
Pronounced "KLUP-per." (Garment-worker slang) noun: an incompetent worker.

KLUTZ
Pronounced "kluts." From the German *Klotz,* "wooden beam" or "blockhead."
1. Noun: a dullard; someone who's always tripping over his own feet.

"I've always enjoyed fooling people with hocus-pocus but I'm such a *klutz* that I have to avoid tricks that involve sleight of hand. My conjuring is based on sleight of mind" (Dr. Crypton, *Dr. Crypton and His Problems*).

Cornbread Maxwell, a forward on the Boston Celtics, told *Inside Sports* (June 1982): "If it's a really bad foul, or if I make a very dumb play, I'll say to myself, 'You made a *klutz* of yourself, Bread. Why'd you go and do that?' "

In *Mad* magazine Don Martin created a superhero named Captain *Klutz*, who was always falling into open manholes. *Klutz* got his name because, as the ill-equipped Ringo Fonebone, he tried to commit suicide by leaping off a tall building but survived when he landed on a fugitive thief.

"*The Nation* has just been sued, for an embarrassingly modest sum, by Harper & Row and *Reader's Digest*—the plaintiffs' claim being that Sticky Fingers (*The Nation*'s editor Victor S. Navasky), in reckless disregard of copyright laws and literary standards, had published material based on a hot manuscript of Gerald Ford's memoirs, which not only failed to be called *The White House Memoirs of a Lucky Klutz*, but failed to be subtitled 'Is This the Fairway for the 8th Hole or What?' " (Calvin Trillin, *The Nation*, April 5, 1980).

2. Adjective (*klutzy*):

"You see all these girls in their twenties who have IQ's of 150 and handle their work so well, but in personal life they're like eight-year-olds. Then you meet a girl who's *klutzy* in her job, but *she* can handle a man" (*Playgirl*, October 1973).

3. Noun (*klutziness*): the state of being *klutzy*.

"A few years ago, he tried to convince me that Sandy Koufax was an Irish kid hired by a cabal under the direction of Arthur J. Goldberg to pretend he was Jewish and thereby end all talk of Jewish *klutziness*" (Calvin Trillin, *The Nation*, July 4, 1981).

KLUTZINESS   See *klutz*.

KLUTZY   See *klutz*.

K'NACKER

Also *k'nocker*. Pronounced "k-NOCK-er." From the German *knacken*, "to crack."
1. Noun: a big shot (someone who cracks the whip).
2. Noun: an old fogy.

KNIP'L   See *knippel*.

KNIPPEL

Also *knip'l*. Pronounced "k-NIP-el." Related to the German *Knopf*, "button."
1. Noun: a button.
2. Noun: money tied in a knot in the corner of a handkerchief; any money stashed away; a nest egg.
3. (Vulgar) noun: hymen; virginity.

KNISH

Pronounced "k-NISH." From the Ukrainian.
1. Noun: a dumpling filled with chopped liver, cheese, potatoes, onions, or buckwheat groats.
2. (Slang) noun: vagina.

> *Knish* appears in *Call It Sleep*, a novel by Henry Roth, who was much taken with Freud's discovery of infant sexuality. In one scene Roth has a young girl try to seduce David Schearl, who is not even six.

> "Yuh know w'ea babies comm from?"
> "N–no."
> "From de *knish*."
> "*Knish?*"
> "Between de legs. Who puts id in is de poppa. De poppa's god de *petzel*. Yaw de poppa."

> The girl then guides David's hand toward her *knish*, but he avoids touching it and flees to his mamma.

> "A stout *yenta* in picador dress but minus leather chaps exchanged a copy of Sara Kasdan's *Love and Knishes* for a poster of Donatello's

David" (S. J. Perelman, "The Joy of Mooching"). *Love and Knishes* is actually a Jewish cookbook. Whereas the play on "love and kisses" was of course intentional, the play on the vulgar slang meaning of *knish* probably escaped the author of the cookbook.

K'NOCKER   See *k'nacker*.

KNOSH   See *nosh*.

KOCHLEFFEL
Also *kochleffl* and *kokhlef'l*. Pronounced "KOKH-lef-full." From the German *kochen*, "to cook," and *Löffel*, "spoon."
Noun: someone who stirs up trouble; a busybody.

"Barbara Walters is a *kochleffel*."

KOCHLEFFL   See *kochleffel*.

KOKHLEF'L   See *kochleffel*.

KOLYIKA   See *kalikeh*.

KOLYIKE   See *kalikeh*.

"MAY YOU GROW LIKE AN ONION
WITH YOUR KOP IN THE GROUND."

KOP

Pronounced "kawp." From the German *Kopf,* "head."
Noun: head.

> There's the Yiddish curse "May you grow like an onion, with
> your *kop* in the ground" and the expression "For you to knock your
> *kop* against the wall, there must be a wall."

KOPTZEN   See *kabtsen.*

"A TOOTHACHE WILL MAKE
YOU FORGET YOUR KOPVAITIK."

KOPVAITIK

Pronounced "KAWP-vay-tick." From the Yiddish *kop,* "head," and the
Yiddish *vaitik,* "pain."
Noun: a headache.

> The homeopathic world view is captured by the Yiddish saying
> "A toothache will make you forget your *kopvaitik.*"

> Adam came to God and said, "Paradise is all well and good, but
> I'm bored. I have no one to talk to."
> God said, "Fine, I'll do something about it," and He created Eve.

A week later Adam called on God again. "Eve is very nice and everything, and talking is all fine and good, but I'm starting to get bored again. Isn't there anything else we can do?"

"Yes, there is," replied God. "You can kiss," and He explained how.

Adam cheered up and disappeared. A week later he returned. "God, kissing is nice, but even that gets to be boring after a while. Isn't there anything else we can do?"

"Why, yes," replied the Supreme Being. "You can fuck," and He explained how.

Adam got all excited and disappeared. A half hour later he was back. "God," he asked, "what's a *kopvaitik*?"

KOSHER
Pronounced "KOH-shur." From the Hebrew *kasher*, "clean," "fit" or "proper."
1. Adjective: fit to eat according to Jewish dietary laws.

> The laws stipulate that only those mammals can be consumed that chew their cud *and* have cloven hooves. Fish can be eaten if they have scales and fins, thus eliminating shellfish from the diet. Meat and milk cannot be consumed at the same meal. Birds of prey are forbidden, as are slithery creatures (snakes, lizards, and what not).

> "Amused, my wife asks why I ordered the *kosher* lunch. 'Because when they bring my chicken dinner this kid with the beard will be in a state,' I explain" (Saul Bellow, *To Jerusalem and Back*).

> "But his eternal *kosher* meat sticks in my throat" (Israel Zangwill, *Children of the Ghetto*, 1892).

2. Adjective: pious.
3. Adjective: aboveboard; proper. Often used in the negative ("not *kosher*") to mean illegitimate.

KOSOKEH   See *kasokeh*.

KRANK
Pronounced "krahnk." From the German *krank*, "sick."
Adjective: ill.

"WHEN A POOR MAN GETS TO EAT A CHICKEN, ONE OF THEM IS KRANK."

A Yiddish proverb has it that "when a poor man gets to eat a chicken, one of them is *krank.*"

KRECHTS

Also *krechtz, krekhts,* and *krekhtz.* Pronounced "krekhts." From the German *krächzen,* "to croak."

1. Exclamation: Sigh!
2. Verb: to groan.
3. Verb: to protest.

Shlomo had just won $1,000,000 in the lottery. Moshe, his neighbor, came over to congratulate him. "Tell me, Shlomo, how did you do it?"

"Well, you see, it was easy. I have two children, Rachel and Esther. Rachel is seven and Esther is six. Seven plus six is fourteen, so I bet on fourteen."

"But," *krechted* Moshe, "seven plus six is thirteen!"

"So who's the mathematician?," asked Shlomo.

KRECHTZ   See *krechts.*

KREKHTS   See *krechts.*

KREKHTZ   See *krechts*.

KREPLACH

Also *kreplakh*. Pronounced "KREP-lakh." From the German *Kreppel*, "fritter."

1. Noun: triangular dumplings filled with meat or cheese; Jewish ravioli.

> "Morris, darling, why don't you stop by for dinner. We're having *kreplach*" (from the movie *No Way to Treat a Lady*, starring George Segal, Lee Remick, and Rod Steiger).

> A Yiddish proverb: "*Kreplach* in a dream are not *kreplach* but a dream."

Sargent Shriver, the Kennedy in-law who replaced the electroshocked Thomas Eagleton as the vice-presidential candidate on the George McGovern ticket in the 1972 elections, was once the director of the Office of Economic Opportunity (OEO). In an interview with *The National Observer*, Shriver described the chief problem of his agency. "You can collect all the ingredients we have here at OEO and examine them one at a time, and everyone shrugs without interest. But you put them all together and call it the 'War on Poverty' and people will look at it and scream 'Yahhhhhh *kreplach*!' "

What did Shriver mean? Well, "Yahhhhhh *kreplach*!" is not only Yiddish but also the punchline of a classic Jewish joke about irrational fear.

A mother tells a psychoanalyst that her son has a deep dread of *kreplach*, small boiled dumplings filled with meat or cheese. The analyst advises her to show the boy exactly how she makes the *kreplach* so that he can see for himself all the ingredients and labor that go into them and realize that there is nothing to fear. The mother decides to follow his advice. She leads the boy into the kitchen and shows him how she rolls the dough and cuts it into little pieces. "This is the same dough that I use in your favorite pancakes. Ummmmmm! It's nothing to be afraid of, is it?"

"No, Mamma."

Next she shows him how she chops the meat for the filling. "Yummy meat. It's nothing to be afraid of, is it?"

"No, Mamma."

Then she spoons the tasty meat onto the squares of his favorite dough. "It's nothing to be afraid of, is it?"

"No, Mamma."

Then she starts to cover the filling with dough. "See. I fold over one corner of the dough like this. And I fold over the second corner like this. Oh so easy! Then I fold the third corner. Nothing to it! Now I take the last corner . . ."

And the boy screams, "Yahhhhhh *kreplach! Kreplach! Kreplach!* "

2. (Slang) noun: nothing; *bubkes.*

KREPLAKH   See *kreplach.*

KUSH

Pronounced "koosh." From the German *Kuss,* "kiss."
Noun: a kiss.

A Yiddish proverb says: "A *kush* from a fool is worse than a blow from a wise man."

KUSHVOKH

Pronounced "koosh-voak." From the Yiddish *kush,* "kiss," and *vokh,* "week."
Noun: a honeymoon.

KUZINA

Pronounced "KOO-zin-ah." From the German *Cousine,* "female cousin."
Noun: a female cousin.

"The butcher, baldish in a stained white smock, looks up from his chopping block. 'Hello, *kuzina,*' he says cheerfully . . . 'Since you say we're related,' she says, laughing, 'why don't I get better cuts of the roast?' " (Ira Berkow, "Happy Endings," New York *Sunday News Magazine,* May 17, 1981).

KVELL

Pronounced "k-VELL." From the German *quellen,* "to gush."
Verb: to be proud; to gloat, especially about the accomplishments of a child.

"Twenty-odd years of nodding and smiling, acknowledging the *kvelling* of the fat ladies who, like the Japanese, are ancestor worshipers" (Jerome Weidman, *Last Respects*).

KVETCH

Pronounced "k-VETCH." From the German *quetschen*, "to squeeze."
1. Verb: to complain; to whine.

"All together now: *kvetch, kvetch, kvetch*. Gripers, whiners and complainers will be encouraged to do just that when Rent-A-Kvetch, the complaint handling service, holds its first *Kvetch*-A-Thon this Saturday in Central Park" ("Sorry Their Lot," *New York Post,* September 17, 1981).

"If my mail is any indication, most bad travel experiences involve the airlines in one way or another. As you might suspect, the individual air carriers vary greatly in the manner in which they respond to customers' *kvetching*" (Stephen Birnbaum, *"Playboy*'s Travel Guide," *Playboy,* November 1981).

"Still, steady *kvetching* will sometimes win the race" (*Family Weekly,* May 2, 1982).

Burt Reynolds has been "known to *kvetch* that, despite his phenomenal drawing power at the box office, the old guard of the film biz doesn't take him seriously enough" (*New York Post,* October 31, 1981).

"Under another ordinance, passed despite some opposition from an organization called Urban Neurotics United, each publisher would be limited to one *Kvetch* Novel per month. ('A *Kvetch* Novel,' in the language of the ordinance, 'will be defined as any novel with a main character to whom any reader might reasonably be expected to say, "Oh, just pull up your socks!" or "Will you please quit *kvetching*?" ')" (Calvin Trillin, *The Nation,* June 24, 1978).

2. Adjective (*kvetchy*): crotchety.

Kirkus Reviews hailed Gail Parent's *The Best Laid Plans* as "Jazzy amusement . . . with sly one-liners and *kvetchy* asides (from Freud, Einstein, and God)."

L'CHAIM See *chaim*.

LEIDEN
Pronounced "LY-den." From the German *leiden*, "to suffer," "to endure."
Verb: to suffer.

LETS See *letz*.

LETZ
Also *lets*. From the Hebrew *letz*, "skeptic."
1. Noun: a cynic.
2. Noun: a comic, prankster, or wit.

LIGNER
Pronounced "LIG-near." From the German *Lügner*, "liar."
Noun: a liar.

> Here are some Yiddish sayings: "If I'm a *ligner*, may I lie with my feet out the door" (in other words, "May I die"); "One lie is a lie, two lies are two lies, and three lies is politics"; and "Half a truth is a whole lie."

LITVAK
Pronounced "LIT-vock."
1. Noun: a Lithuanian Jew.
2. Noun: a clever but insensitive person.
3. (Vulgar) noun: a swindler. This is a racial slur.

LOCH
Pronounced "LAWKH." From the German *Loch*, "hole" or "orifice."
1. Noun: a hole.
2. (Vulgar) noun: vagina.

LOKSH

Pronounced "lucksh." Plural is *lokshen.*
1. Noun: a noodle.

> "In Beijing, China, Rachel hoped the dish was *lokshen,* but it was actually sea worms."

2. Noun: a thin person; someone as thin as a noodle.

> "Shlomo is such a *loksh* that he has to jump around in the shower to get wet."

3. Noun: Italian.

LOKSHEN   See *loksh.*

LOZ IM GAYN

Pronounced "LAW-zem-GA-in." Literally, "let him go."
Phrase: Let him go! What do you need him for? Forget it!

> In Mel Brooks's movie *Blazing Saddles,* an Indian chief orders his men, who have surrounded a black man, to *"Loz im gayn."*

LUFTMENSH

LUFTMENSH

Pronounced "luft" as in "Lufthansa" and "mensh" to rhyme with "quench." From the German *Luft*, "air," and *Mensch*, "man."
1. Noun: a "man of the air"; someone who has his head in the clouds; a dreamer.

> "No *luftmensh* he, but a *golem* [automaton], pure and simple" (Wallace Markfield's review of Myron Kaufmann's *Remember Me to God*, in *Commentary*, November 1957).

2. Noun: someone who doesn't have a job who wanders aimlessly.

LUMP

From the German *Lump*, "rascal."
Noun: a scoundrel.

M

MACHER

Pronounced "MA-kher." From the German *machen,* "to make" or "to do."

1. Noun: someone who is going places; a wheeler-dealer.

> "[Jacobo Timerman] was something of a *macher* in those days, a maker and doer, proud of his contacts with powerful and influential men" (Michael Walzer's review of Jacobo Timerman's *Prisoner Without a Name, Cell Without a Number,* in the *New York Review of Books,* May 29, 1981).

2. Noun: someone who has gone places; a big shot; the boss.

> "Do I look sharp, bright, successful, a *macher?*" (John Jacob Clayton, *What Are Friends For?*)

> "It doesn't matter a tinker's cuss whether you amend the constitution to call the chairman president, *macher* or grand panjandrum" (*Jewish Guardian,* February 2, 1963).

MAIDEL

Also *maydele* and *meyd'l.* Pronounced "MAY-dull" or "MAY-dull-ah." From the German *Mädel,* "girl."

1. Noun: a young girl.

> "The *maydele* gives him a little hug, as if to say, 'Notice me, pay attention!'" (Wallace Markfield, *To an Early Grave*)

> A Yiddish saying goes: "If a *maidel* can't dance, she says the band can't play."

2. Noun: a virgin.

MAIVIN   See *maven.*

MAKE

Also *makeh* and *makkes*. Pronounced "mach-eh" or "mach-ess." From the Hebrew *makah*, "plague."
1. Noun: plague.
2. Noun: nothing; *bubkes*.

MAKEH   See *make*.

MAKKES   See *make*.

MALACH

Also *malakh* and *moloch*. Pronounced "MA-lakh." From the Hebrew *malakh*, "angel."
Noun: an angel.

> In *The Implosion Conspiracy*, Louis Nizer describes Julius Rosenberg's first impression of Ethel: "He had abandoned his religious beliefs but emotions are no respecter of rational processes. She looked like a *moloch*."

MALACH-HAMOVES

Also *malakhamoves* and *melech-hamovess*. Pronounced "MAL-ach-HA-mohv-ess." From the Hebrew *malakh hamavet*, "angel of death."
1. Noun: the male angel of death.

> "Only send a lazy person for the *malach-hamoves*" is a proverbial warning.

2. Noun (*malach-hamovesteh*): a bad wife.

MALACH-HAMOVESTEH   See *malach-hamoves*.

MALAKH   See *malach*.

MALAKHAMOVES   See *malach-hamoves*.

MAMZER   See *momzer*.

MAVEN

Also *maivin, mavin, mayvin,* and *meyvin.* Pronounced "MAY-ven." From the Hebrew *mevin,* "someone who understands."
1. Noun: an expert; a connoisseur.

In 1978 *The New York Times* applauded the Girl Scout who sold the most cookies that year. The headline called her "The Cookie *Mavin.*"

"There I was, happily *shlepping* pizzas to a steady and growing clientele of pizza *mavins,* when all of a sudden *The Underground Gourmet* and *New York* magazine named my little pizza store as the best in New York" (*New York,* June 15, 1970).

"Rubik's Cube *mavens* should consult this book" (Dr. Crypton, *Dr. Crypton and His Problems*).

"Horror *mavens* like Madeline Kahn . . ." (*New York Post,* October 14, 1981).

2. (Garment-worker slang) noun: a customer who thinks he knows more than the tailor does about clothes.

MAVIN   See *maven.*

MAYDELE   See *maidel.*

MAYVIN   See *maven.*

MAZEL

Also *mazol.* Pronounced "MA-zull." From the Hebrew *mazal,* "luck."
1. Noun: luck.

"Better a little *mazel* than a lot of gold" is an old adage.

2. Exclamation (*Mazel tov!*): Congratulations! (Literally, "Good luck!")

"When He wills, walls of iron must give way. It is a divine match —anyone can see it is. May they live a hundred and twenty years together. *Mazol-tov!*" (Abraham Cahan, "The Imported Bridegroom," 1898).

"Someone in the crowd shouted '*Mazel tov*!' and the words were picked up by the others until they became an ecstatic din" (Chaim Potok, *The Promise*).

MAZOL   See *mazel.*

MAZOOMA   See *mezuma.*

MAZUMA   See *mezuma.*

MAZUME   See *mezuma.*

MECHULEH
Also *mechulle* and *mekhule.* Pronounced "m-KHOOL-uh." From the Hebrew *mekhulah,* "ended."
Noun or adjective: failed; spoiled; aborted; out of order; bankrupt.

MECHULLE   See *mechuleh.*

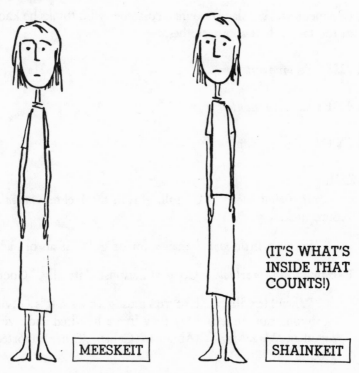

(IT'S WHAT'S INSIDE THAT COUNTS!)

MEESKEIT   SHAINKEIT

MEESKEIT

Also *meeskite* and *mieskeit*. Pronounced "MEES-kite." From the Yiddish *mies*, "ugly."
Noun: an ugly person or thing.

> "Not only that, but you're stupid, your wife's a *meeskeit* and if you don't get off my foot you're excommunicated" (Woody Allen, *Getting Even*).

MEESKITE   See *meeskeit*.

MEGILE   See *megillah*.

MEGILLAH

Also *megile*. Pronounced "muh-GILL-uh." From the Hebrew *megillah*, "scroll."
1. Noun: a long story. The *Megillah* is the biblical Book of Esther, which is quite long.
2. Noun: a rigmarole.

MEKHULE   See *mechuleh*.

MELAMED

Pronounced "mull-LAH-mud." From the Hebrew *melamed*, "teacher."
1. Noun: a teacher of religion or Hebrew.

> "He became a dead ringer for my old *melamed*, Rabbi Goldfarb on Columbia Street. An absolute dead ringer, including the obsequious smile reserved for parents in the throes of negotiating the price of a bar mitzvah" (Jerome Weidman, *Tiffany Street*).

2. Noun: a wise man.
3. Noun: a parochial bore. Someone who is too "bookish" to notice what's going on around him.

MELECH-HAMOVESS   See *malach-hamoves*.

MENCH   See *mensh*.

MENSCH   See *mensh*.

MENSH

MENSH

Also *mench, mensch,* and *mentsch.* Pronounced "mench." From the German *Mensch,* "human being."
Noun: an admirable human being; a person of great dignity; the finest specimen of our species.

> Stephen Spielberg said of his creation E.T.: "He's a squashy little *mensch,* the kind of guy you want to take home to mother."

> "Loveable wench seeks sensitive *mensch*" (a classified ad in the "Personal" section of the *New York Review of Books,* June 24, 1982).

> "So what do you do to get rid of a cold? You go out like a *mentsch* in the street and breathe, 'Ahhh,' the fresh air, you go among people and make out nothing's the matter and God helps and the cold is gone" (Karl Fruchtmann, "A Man on His Back").

> "You're not like those other university phonies. You're a *mensch*" (Saul Bellow, *Herzog*).

> When Jewish kids *shlump* over the dinner table, their fathers say, "Sit up like a *mensh.*"

MENTSCH   See *mensh.*

MESCHUGGE   See *meshugge.*

MESHPOCHEH   See *mishpocheh.*

MESHUGAS   See *mishegoss.*

MESHUGE   See *meshugge.*

MESHUGEH   See *meshugge.*

MESHUGGE
Also *meschugge, meshuge,* and *meshugeh.* Pronounced "m-SHU-guh."
From the Hebrew *meshugah,* "crazy."
1. Adjective: crazy; mad.

"Then I heard she became absolutely stark raving *meshugeh;* what
happened was she tried to do a synthesis of Marx and Freud and she
found out she would have to read Marx and Freud" (Wallace
Markfield, *Teitlebaum's Window*).

In letters to Wilhelm Fliess, the Berlin nose-and-throat surgeon,
Freud "refers affectionately to his children as '*Fratzen*' and '*Wörmen*'
—brats and worms—and sprinkles around an occasional '*meschugge*'" ("Hidden Freud Is Sought in Unpublished Letters," *The
New York Times,* August 18, 1981).

" 'Are you *meshuggah*?' she asked with an awful silence. 'Or have
you, perhaps, saved up a tidy sum of money?' " (Israel Zangwill,
Children of the Ghetto, 1892).

About 1930 a song was popular in New York public schools. One
line went: "I'm crazy about my sugar, and my sugar's *meshugge*
for me."

"He [John Berryman] deleted a few of the sections I marked
'psycho-*meshuge*' (a bastard-Yiddish term we used in Princeton for
a woman in town who was so humorlessly Freudian that she
analyzed even her dog's bark)" (Eileen Simpson, *Poets in Their
Youth*).

2. Noun (*meshuggener* or *meshugginer* for a man; *meshuggeneh* or *meshuggina* for a woman): a madman.

A few days after the Israelis bombed the Iraqi reactor, Prime Minister Menachem Begin was interviewed on American television. What would he do, a reporter asked him, if Libyan strong man Qaddafi built a nuclear reactor. "Please," Begin replied, "one *meshuggener* at a time."

MESHUGGENEH   See *meshugge*.

MESHUGGENER   See *meshugge*.

MESHUGGINA   See *meshugge*.

MESHUGGINER   See *meshugge*.

MESHUMAD   See *meshumed*.

MESHUMED
Also *meshumad*. Pronounced "m-SHOE-med." From the Hebrew *meshumad*, "a destroyed one."
Noun: a Jew who has converted to Christianity.

METSIAH   See *metsieh*.

METSIEH
Also *metsiah*, *metsiye*, and *mitsiah*. Pronounced "met-SEE-yeh." From the Hebrew *metziah*, "a find."
1. Noun: a find; a bargain; a great discovery.

A Yiddish proverb tells us: "Life is the greatest *metsieh*—you get it for nothing."
2. (Sarcastic) noun: a real prize.

"As islands go, the Falklands are a *metsieh*."

On the television show *Your Show of Shows*, Sid Caesar called a Japanese houseboy "Takeh Metsieh," as a twist on the name of the composer Toru Takemitsu.

3. (Idiomatic) noun: deal, as in "So what's the big *metsieh*?"

METSIYE   See *metsieh.*

MEYD'L   See *maidel.*

MEYVIN   See *maven.*

MEZUMA
Also *mazooma, mazuma,* and *mazume.* Pronounced "m-ZOOM-ah."
From the Hebrew *mezuman,* "ready" or "fixed."
Noun: money.

> "I don't know where the Rumfords got their money, but they
> don't have to work at all, I know that. They just sit on that porch
> there, and drink martinis, and let the old *mazooma* roll in" (Kurt
> Vonnegut, Jr., "The Hyannis Port Story").

MEZUZAH   See *mezuze.*

MEZUZE
Also *mezuzah.* Pronounced "meh-ZOO-zuh." From the Hebrew *mezu-
zah,* "doorpost."
Noun: a scroll containing the ancient credo "Hear, O Israel, the Lord our
God, the Lord is One" that Jews attach to the right-hand post of every
door of the house as an affirmation of faith.

> "My sons worked hard to earn a piece of bread, because inscribing
> *mezuzahs* doesn't bring much of an income. . . ." (Isaac Bashevis
> Singer, "The Lecture").

MIES
Pronounced "meace." From the German *mies,* "wretched."
Adjective: ugly.

MIESKEIT   See *meeskeit.*

MIESSE MESHINA
Also *mise meshone.* Pronounced "MEE-sa-ma-SHE-nah." From the Hebrew *mitah meshunah,* "violent death." Also influenced by the Yiddish
mies, "ugly."
Noun: an ugly death.

MIESSE MESHINA

MIKVA See *mikvah*.

MIKVAH

Also *mikva* and *mikveh*. Pronounced "MICK-vuh." From the Hebrew *mikvah*, "well" or "pool."
Noun: a ritual bath. Used by converts to Judaism, by married women seven days after each menstrual period, and by women who have just given birth.

"An Israeli woman is required to go to a *mikvah* before her wedding—and it is estimated that 90 percent of the women in this unorthodox country comply . . . A woman who does not want to go to a *mikvah* has two choices: she can bribe someone to sign a paper saying she has been to one, or she can go to Cyprus to be married by a justice of the peace. This practice has become so commonplace of late that the leader of Cyprus is often referred to as Rabbi Makarios" (Nora Ephron, "Women in Israel: The Myth of Liberation," *Crazy Salad*).

MIKVEH See *mikvah*.

MILCHIKER

MILCHIGER   See *milchik*.

MILCHIK

Pronounced "MIL-shick." From the German *Milch*, "milk."
1. Adjective: used to describe foods that contain milk and therefore cannot be eaten with meat in accordance with Jewish dietary laws.

> "We also took books and magazines from stock and read them upstairs at meals. Mom complained that we spilled food on them. 'Did you make that book *milchik* or *fleishik* ["meat-containing"]?' she would ask bitterly" (Rose A. Englander, "The Jewish Stationery Store," *Commentary*, May 1946).

2. Adjective: weak.
3. Noun (*milchiger* or *milchiker*): Caspar Milquetoast.

MILCHIKER   See *milchik*.

MINYAN

Also *minyon*. Pronounced "MIN-yun." From the Hebrew *minyan*, "number" or "reckoning."
1. Noun: the ten men needed to have a religious service.

"This was twenty-seven years ago, and at that time there were not enough Americans in Majorca to provide even an illegal *minyan*" ("Letters from Readers," *Commentary,* March 1957).

"Rabbi Wachtfogel is, of course, correct in stating that circumcision, marriage, and burial rites are *legally* valid without the presence of a *minyan*" ("Letters from Readers," *Commentary,* July 1959).

2. Noun: a quorum.

MINYON   See *minyan.*

MISE MESHONE   See *miesse meshina.*

MISHBAWKHA   See *mishpocheh.*

MISHEGAAS   See *mishegoss.*

MISHEGOSS
Also *meshugas* and *mishegaas.* Pronounced "mish-eh-GOSS." From the Hebrew *meshugah,* "crazy."
Noun: insanity.

MISH-MASH   See *mish-mosh.*

MISH-MOSH
Also *mish-mash.* Pronounced "mish-mosh." From the German *Mischmasch,* "hotchpotch."
1. Noun: a hotchpotch

"All in all, a very fine reception for a, let's be frank, a rather trumped-up *mishmash* of a book" (John Updike, *Bech: A Book*).

2. Noun: confusion; crossed signals; a mess.

MISHPAHAH   See *mishpocheh.*

MISHPAWKHA   See *mishpocheh.*

MISHPOCHA See *mishpocheh.*

MISHPOCHEH
Also *meshpocheh, mishbawkha, mishpahah, mishpawkha,* and *mishpocha.*
Pronounced "mish-PAW-cha." From the Hebrew *mishpahah,* "family."
Noun: an extended family; all one's relatives.

> "Members of the *mishpocheh* were always welcome at any and
> all of the Lewisohn houses, and at times the troupe of followers
> grew so large that if a friend didn't keep careful track of his host's
> next-day plans, it was easy to get left behind" (Stephen Birming-
> ham, *"Our Crowd": The Great Jewish Families of New York).*

> "It has an arched eyebrow for the equally poor but dishonest
> black sheep of the *mishpocha*—the bare-looking store, thinly
> stocked, which fronts for a backroom bookie place and fools no-
> body, not even the police" (Rose A. Englander, "The Jewish Statio-
> nery Store," *Commentary,* May 1946).

MITSIAH See *metsieh.*

MITTELMESSIG See *muttelmessig.*

MITTELMESSIKER
Pronounced "MIT-tell-MESS-i-ker." From the German *Mittel,* "average," and *Messe,* "mess."
1. Noun: the average person; the common man; John Doe; Joe Shmo.
2. Noun: hoi polloi.

MOEL See *moyl.*

MOHEL See *moyl.*

MOISHE KAPOYR
Also *Moyshe Kapoyr.* Pronounced "MOY-shuh-ca-POYR." From the
Yiddish *Moishe,* "Moses," and the Russian *kubaryom,* "reversed." Liter-
ally, "Moses reversed."

> The expression comes from a cartoon character named *Moishe
> Kapoyr* in the *Jewish Daily Forward* in the 1920's.

MOISHE KAPOYR

1. Noun: Mr. Upside Down. Someone who always puts the cart before the horse, swims against the tide, and marches to a different drummer.
2. Noun: someone who is contrary, who always does the opposite of what you want.

MOLOCH See *malach.*

MOMZER

Also *mamzer* and *mumzer.* Pronounced "MOM-zir." From the Hebrew *mamzer,* "bastard."
1. Noun: an illegitimate child. In Judaism this includes a child born of a religiously mixed marriage or of an incestuous marriage.
2. Noun: a despicable individual; a "bastard."

> "Yes, at an early age I knew all about Father Coughlin, about the German Bund groups and Henry Ford. Because of him our pickups were always Chevys. 'Not a dollar to such an anti-Semitic *momzer,*' Momma said. 'Never a Ford, not even a used one' " (Max Apple, *Zip*).

> The Yiddish adage "When a mother calls her child '*momzer,*' you can believe her" means "Trust a mother to know her own child."

3. Noun: a shrewd con man.

4. (Shoestore slang): someone who spends a lot of time in one shoestore but buys a pair of shoes in a neighboring store.

MOYL

Also *moel* and *mohel*. Pronounced "moil." From the Hebrew *mohel*, "ritual circumciser."

Noun: one who performs circumcisions.

MOYSHE KAPOYR   See *Moishe Kapoyr*.

MUMZER See *momzer.*

MUTEK

Pronounced "MOO-tick." From the German *mutig,* "brave."
Adjective: brave.

MUTTELMESSIG

Also *mittelmessig.* Pronounced "MIT-tell-MESS-ick." From the German
Mittel, "middle," and *Messe,* "mess."
Noun: someone who makes a mess in the middle; a *kibbitzer.*

NAAR See *nar.*

NAARISHKEIT See *nar.*

NACHSHLEPPER See *nochshlepper.*

NADAN

Pronounced "NOD-en." From the Hebrew *nadan,* "dowry."
Noun: a dowry.

NAFISH See *nayfish.*

NAFKEH

Pronounced "NAF-cuh." From the Aramaic.
Noun: a prostitute.

NAR

Also *naar.* Pronounced "nar." From the German *Narr,* "fool," "clown,"
or "buffoon." The plural is *naromin* or *nars.*
1. Noun: a fool.

> The *nar* is the subject of many Yiddish sayings. "When a wise
> man talks to a *nar,* two *naromin* are talking." "When a *nar* goes to
> the baths, he forgets to clean his face." "When a *nar* holds a cow
> by the horns, a wise man can milk her." "A dead man is mourned
> for seven days; a *nar,* for his whole life." "Grind a *nar* in a pepper
> grinder and he'll think you meant to grind not him but the pepper."

2. Adjective (*narish*): foolish.
3. Noun (*naarishkeit, narishkeit,* and *narrishchkeit*): foolishness.

"They believe any *Narrishkeit*! I and you are the only two sensible Jews in England" (Israel Zangwill, *Children of the Ghetto*, 1892).

NARISH   See *nar*.

NARISHKEIT   See *nar*.

NARRISCHKEIT   See *nar*.

NASH   See *nosh*.

NAYFISH
Also *nafish* and *nefish*. Pronounced "NAY-fish." From the Hebrew *nefesh*, "person."
Noun: someone who is pathetic or inconsequential; someone you always forget to introduce at a party.

NEB
Pronounced "neb." From the Yiddish *nebbish*, "nobody."
Noun: a nobody; a sad sap.

NEBBECH   See *nebbish*.

NEBBICH   See *nebbish*.

NEBBISH
Also *nebbech, nebbich, nebech,* and *nebish.* Pronounced "NEB-bish." From the Czechoslovakian.
1. Noun: a nobody; a loser; a drip. There is also the further diminutive *nebechel.*

> "It looks like Pa isn't anything like the *nebbish* Ma is always making him out to be" (G. Millstein, *The New York Times Book Review,* October 7, 1951).

2. Adjective (also *nebbishe* and *nebbisher*): ineffectual; hapless.

> "The central character is so *nebbish* he has not even a name" (*The New York Times,* April 6, 1968).

> "Paranoid psychopaths who, after *nebbish* lives, suddenly feel themselves invulnerable in the certain wooing of sweet death" (*Atlantic Monthly,* September 1969).

3. Interjection: Unfortunately!

NEBBISHE   See *nebbish*.

NEBBISHER   See *nebbish*.

NEBECH   See *nebbish*.

NEBECHEL   See *nebbish*.

NEBISH   See *nebbish*.

NECHTIGER TOG
Pronounced "NEKH-tick-er-TOG" (rhymes with "log"). From the German *Nacht,* "night," and *Tag,* "day." Literally, "a nightly day."
Noun: an impossibility.

NEFISH   See *nayfish*.

NEKAIVEH

Also *nekeyve*. Pronounced "NE-kay-veh." From the Hebrew *nekevah*, "woman."
1. Noun: a woman.
2. Noun: a woman of low morals; a prostitute.

NEKEYVE See *nekaiveh*.

NESHOMELEH

Pronounced "nesh-OHM-e-luh." From the Hebrew *neshamah*, "soul." Literally, "little soul."
Noun: sweetheart.

SIKORSKY

OPSTAIRSIKEH

YOU

NEXDOOREKEH

DONSTAIRSIKEH

NEXTDOORSIKEH

Pronounced "neks-DOOR-si-kuh."
Noun: the female neighbor next door.

In a Truffaut film, Gérard Depardieu gets hopelessly entangled with Fanny Arendt, the *nextdoorsikeh*.

-NICK   See *-nik*.

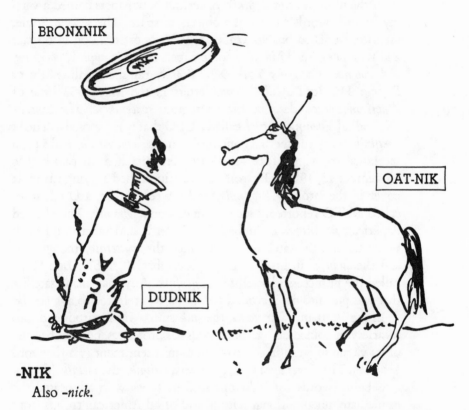

-NIK
Also *-nick*.

A Slavic personifying suffix which can mean "a devotee of" or "an ardent practitioner of." Found in such Yiddish words as *nudnik* (a devotee of *noodging*) and *kasnik* (a devotee of heat—a hothead). Although Yinglish *-nik* words such as *alrightnik, nogoodnik,* and *holdupnik* appear frequently in American fiction, they are not the products of a novelist's comic imagination. (See the individual entries for these three words.) They were coined by Jewish immigrants to this country from the first American English idioms they learned. Immigrants were also responsible for *realestatenik* and *lodgenick*.

The popularity of the *-nik* suffix in English is largely due to the

Soviet *Sputnik*, the first man-made satellite, launched on October 4, 1957. (In Russian, *put* means "road" and *s* is a preposition that means "along" or "with"; thus *sputnik*—literally, "along the roader"—is a companion or a satellite.)

In the months after *Sputnik* American newspapers coined a variety of *-nik* words to describe objects in space. The second Soviet satellite, launched on November 3, 1957, boosted a dog into space and was nicknamed *Muttnik;* some papers called it *pupnik, poochnik,* and *woofnik.* The New York *Daily Worker* ran the headline "Every *Dognik* Has Its *Daynik.*" Two letters in the May 1958 issue of *American Speech* describe the contagious *spacenikese. The Lincoln* [Nebraska] *Evening Journal* called a UFO that was exposed as a hoax a *puffnik,* a toy rocket that contained a mouse a *mousenik,* and a local racehorse to which fake antennae were attached an *oatnik.* On November 13, 1957, a Detroit radio station called a flying manhole cover in the Bronx a *Bronxnik,* and a week before, a U.P.I. story called a UFO reportedly seen by an ex-con a *whatnik.* The planned American satellite was dubbed the *Yanknik;* and when the launch was a failure, the satellite was renamed the *sputternik,* the *pfudnik,* and the *dudnik.* In his TV show (December 10, 1957), Bob Hope called the unsuccessful satellite the *goofnik.* Any man-made satellite that was put into orbit around the moon was referred to as a *lunnik.*

In the Vietnam War years, the *-nik* suffix was incorporated into a variety of coined derogatory words for protesters, perhaps because of its vague suggestion of pro-Communist sentiment (via the word *Sputnik*). There were *peacenik, protestnik, quitnik,* and *vietnik* (the last two being words for unkempt student types who advocated the immediate, unconditional withdrawal of all American troops from Vietnam). And there were *discothequenik, dopenik,* and *folknik* (a lover of folk music). On the record *A Way of Life,* Mort Sahl says, "He lost all his money—a *weirdnik.*"

Today we have *refusenik,* the word for a Soviet Jew who has been refused an exit visa. (See, for example, the book *Refusenik: Trapped in the Soviet Union* by Mark Ya. Azbel.)

NISHTGUTNIK

Pronounced "nisht-GOOT-nick." From the German *nicht,* "not," and *gut,* "good."

Noun: a good-for-nothing.

NISHTIKEIT

Pronounced "NISH-ti-kite." From the German *Nichtigkeit,* "nothing-ness."
Noun: a nobody.

NOCHSHLEPPER

Also *nachshlepper.* Pronounced "NAWKH-shlepper." From the German *noch,* "after," and the Yiddish *shlepper,* "one who drags himself around."
Noun: someone who follows after; a hanger-on.

> "Am I the *primum mobiles,* am I more than a *nachshlepper* in the order of things?" (Wallace Markfield, *To an Early Grave*).

NOGOODNICK   See *nogoodnik.*

NOGOODNIK

Also *nogoodnick.* Pronounced "no-GOOD-nick." (See the entry for *-nik.*)
1. Noun: a person to be avoided, for whatever reason; someone who is "no good."

> In the cartoon strip "Li'l Abner," Al Capp introduced a *nogood-nik,* a fierce, malicious animal that it is best to avoid.

2. Noun: a bum.

> "A parasite, a leech, a bloodsucker—altogether a five-star *nogood-nik!*" (S. J. Perelman, "Waiting for Santy").

NOODGE

Also *noudge, nudj, nudje,* and *nudzh.* Pronounced "noodj." From the Slavic *nudyen,* "to bore."
1. Noun: a nagger; a badgerer.

> "A man journeyed to Chelm in order to seek the advice of Rabbi Ben Kaddish, the holiest of all ninth-century rabbis and perhaps the greatest *noudge* of the medieval era" (Woody Allen, *Getting Even*).

2. Verb: to nag; to pester.
3. Adjective (*nudzhedik* or *nudzhik*): nagged to death; nauseous.

NOSH

Also *knosh* and *nash*. Pronounced "nosh." From the German *nachen*, "to nibble" or "to snack."

1. Verb: to snack; to nibble; to eat a small bit of.

"So what do you want from me, I like to *knosh*. A little chopped liver, a little smoked fish. . . ." (Herbert Selby, Jr., *Requiem for a Dream*).

2. Noun: a snack; a tidbit; a "little something."

Bagel *Nosh* is a popular chain of snack spots.

3. Noun (*nosher*): someone who nibbles.

"While you (the Pac-Man or his Ms.) are 'doing-in' dots, four speedy spooks are trying to tackle you! And who are these notorious *noshers*?" (Jews for Jesus, "Pac-Man Fever").

NOSHER   See *nosh*.

NOUDGE   See *noodge*.

NU

Pronounced "noo." From the Russian.
Exclamation: Well! So!

"You think a friend is an easy thing to be? If you are truly his friend, you will discover otherwise. We will see. *Nu*, it is too late and your father is certainly worried that you are away so long" (Chaim Potok, *The Chosen*).

"*Nu*, how shall I tell you how glad we were after eleven days on the empty ocean we saw the buildings of New York?" (Michael Gold, "Sam Kravitz, That Thief").

NUDJ   See *noodge*.

NUDJE   See *noodge*.

NUDNICK   See *nudnik*.

NUDNIK

NUDNIK

Also *nudnick*. The first syllable rhymes with "hood." From the Russian *nudna*, which, according to Nathan Ausubel, can be freely translated as "It's enough to throw up."
Noun: a colossal, talkative bore.

> "Just because Bill married a *nudnick* who reads F. Scott Fitzgerald do I have to play the Bohemian in my old age? Nude croquet! I don't know which is worse, the nude or the croquet!" (Leslie Fiedler, "Nude Croquet").

> "The patrons of New York's Ruben Bleu are as boorish a collection of *nudnicks* as ever assembled in a public place" (*New Republic*, April 14, 1947).

> "It makes no difference to me if these *nudnicks* happen to be atheists" (*Commentary*, December 10, 1950).

NUDZH   See *noodge*.

NUDZHEDIK   See *noodge*.

NUDZHIK   See *noodge*.

OI See *oy.*

OLREITNIK See *alrightnik.*

ONGEBLOZZEN
Pronounced "AWN-ge-blass-en." From the German *blasen,* "to puff."
1. Adjective: puffed up; conceited.
2. Adjective: peevish.
3. Noun (*ongeblozzener*): an arrogant person.

ONGEBLOZZENER See *ongeblozzen.*

ONGESHTOPT
Pronounced "AWN-ge-shtupt." From the German *stopfen,* "to stuff."
Literally, "stuffed up."
Adjective: overstuffed; super-rich.

ONGETRUNKEN
Pronounced "AWN-ge-trunk-en." From the German *trinken,* "to drink."
Adjective: drunk; soused.

OPSTAIRSIKEH

Pronounced "op-STAIR-zi-kuh."
1. Noun: a female upstairs neighbor.
2. Noun (*opstairsiker*): a male upstairs neighbor.

OPSTAIRSIKER   See *opstairsikeh*.

OY

Also *oi*. Pronounced like the "oy" in "boy."
Exclamation: Oh!

> " '*Oi* a lamentation upon me! He shaves his beard!' Gitl ejaculated to herself as she scrutinized her husband" (Abraham Cahan, *Yekl*, 1896).

OYSGAMITCHED

Pronounced "OYS-ga-mitched."
Adjective: totally worn out.

> "Over a year we tried and tried till I was *oysgamitched*, and that was the night" (Philip Roth, *Goodbye Columbus*).

OYSGEMATERT

Pronounced "oys-ge-MA-tairt." From the German *ermatten*, "to exhaust or wear down."
Adjective: fatigued.

OYSGEMUTSHET

Pronounced "OYS-ge-moo-chet." From the Slavic *mutshen*, "to torment."
Adjective: tormented to distraction; tortured.

OYSGEPUTST   See *oysgeputzt*.

OYSGEPUTZT

Also *oysgeputst*. Pronounced "OYS-ge-putst." From the German *putzen*, "to dress," "to adorn."
Adjective: overdressed.

OYSVORF

Also *oysvurf.* Pronounced "OYS-voff." From the German *Auswurf,* "trash."

1. Noun: an outcast; an outsider.
2. Noun: a nasty *kibbitzer.*

OYSVURF   See *oysvorf.*

OYTSER

Pronounced "OYT-sir." From the Hebrew *otsar,* "treasure."
1. Noun: a treasure.
2. (Sarcastic) noun: a real treasure.

There is the mild curse "I'll bury him like an *oytser.*"

PARECH

Also *par'kh*. Pronounced "PAR-ekh." From the Slavic for "mange of the scalp."
1. Noun: a wretched disease in which one sprouts scales on the head.
2. Noun: someone suffering from this disease.
3. Noun: a shady, disgusting character.

PAR'KH   See *parech*.

PARNOSE   See *parnosseh*.

PARNOSSEH

Also *parnose*. Pronounced "par-NUSS-eh." From the Hebrew *parnasah*, "livelihood."
Noun: livelihood.

  The truth about *parnosseh* is embodied in a couple of Yiddish folk sayings: "If people could hire others to do their dying, the poor would have a good *parnosseh*" and "An attractive wife is half a *parnosseh*."

PARTATSHNEK

Pronounced "par-TATSH-neck."
Adjective: shoddy.

PASKUDNAK   See *paskudne*.

PASKUDNE

Also *paskudneh*. Pronounced "pass-COOD-neh." From the Polish "disgusting."
1. Adjective: revolting; unmentionably ugly.

Shlomo was so depressed that he consulted a psychoanalyst. After a fifty-minute session the analyst concluded: "There's no doubt about it. You're extremely disturbed." Shlomo said he wanted to get a second opinion. "Second opinion?," the shrink replied, "OK, You're *paskudne,* too."

2. Noun (*paskudnak, paskudnik,* and *paskudnyak*): an odious person.

"Energetically bundling her and Misty, the poodle, into the car, I presented the onlookers with a small token of Italo-American amity—to wit, the evil eye—and, springing behind the wheel ere they could reciprocate, made for the pier where the S.S. *Pascudnik,* our carrier to Dubrovnik, lay berthed" (S. J. Perelman, "Misty Behind the Curtain").

PASKUDNEH   See *paskudne.*

PASKUDNIK   See *paskudne.*

PASKUDNYAK   See *paskudne.*

PATCH   See *patsh.*

PATSH

Also *patch, potch,* and *potsh.* Pronounced "potch." From the German *Patsch,* "a slap in the face" or "a box on the ear."
1. Noun: a slap.

A Yiddish adage says: "A *patsh* will always heal but a harsh word will always be remembered."

2. Verb: to slap.

"My mother . . . *potched* my face after I was a married woman. I shall never forget that slap—it nearly made me adhere to the wall" (Israel Zangwill, *Children of the Ghetto,* 1892).

PATSHER   See *patshken.*

PATSHKEN

Also *potshken.* Pronounced "POTSH-ken." From the German *patschen,* "to splash or paddle about."

1. Verb: to work in a half-assed way. Often used as in *"patshkied around."*

> "I feed the goldfish, I make a few *latkes* [potato pancakes], I paint the kitchen chairs, I stuff the hassock Morty Zelenke got me from Tangiers, I *potske* with my pottery" (Wallace Markfield, *To an Early Grave*).

2. Noun (*patsher*): an idler; a lazy worker.

PATSHER   See *patshken.*

PATSHKIED AROUND   See *patshken.*

PETSEL
Also *petzel.* Pronounced "PET-sell." Diminutive of the Yiddish *putz,* "penis."
Noun: penis.

> S. J. Perelman often used Yiddish words for the names of his characters: "Physically, Professor Pitzel was unimpressive; a troglodyte just over four feet in height, he was myopic, ill-favored, and snappish, but he was engaged in a wonderful experiment. From deep in Lake Titicaca, on the Peru-Bolivia border, he had retrieved a family of salamanders, creatures that had been sightless for two hundred million years, and was grafting eyes onto them" ("Methinks the Lady Doth Propel Too Much").

PETSELEH
Also *petzula.* Pronounced "PET-sell-uh." Diminutive of the Yiddish *putz,* "penis."
Noun: little penis.

> "In Ancient Greece *petselehs* were the mark of masculine beauty. Times have changed."

PETZEL   See *petsel.*

PETZULA   See *petseleh.*

Ph.G

Ph.G.

Rhymes with "Ph.D." Acronym for "Papa has *gelt* (money)."
Phrase: Daddy has big bucks.

PHUDNIK

Pronounced "FUD-nick," in which "fud" rhymes with "wood." Portmanteau of the English *Ph.D.* and the Yiddish *nudnik*, "bore."
Noun: an overly studious doctoral candidate.

    English has no comparable word even though it has a host of slang words for a boring undergraduate who studies too much: *wonk, grind, weanie, nerd, squid,* and so on.

PIPIK   See *pupik.*

PISHECHTZ   See *pishen.*

PISHEN

Pronounced "pishen." From the German *pissen*, "to urinate."
1. Verb: to piss.

    "They both *pish* in the same pot" is a Yiddish expression that means "they're inseparable."

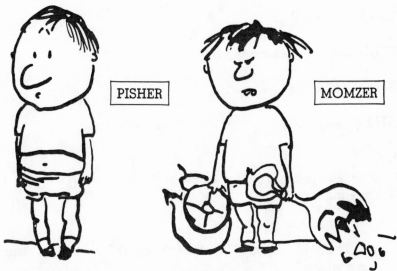

2. Noun (*pisher* for males; *pisherkeh* for females): a little squirt; a term of endearment for an infant.

> "Coffee and a doughnut, and on this a thirteen-year-old *pisher* with half a stomach is supposed to start a day" (Philip Roth, *Portnoy's Complaint*).

3. Noun (*pisherel*): a very little squirt.
4. (Vulgar) noun (*pisher* for males; *pisherkeh* for females): a nobody, someone of no consequence.

> In Bernard Malamud's *The Assistant,* Helen Bober turns down Louis Karp's marriage proposal because she doesn't want a store-keeper for a husband. Louis responds, "Wines and liquors aren't exactly *pisher* groceries."

> The defiant command *"Ruf mich pisher* (literally, "call me pisser") means "Say what you want; sticks and stones may break my bones but names will never hurt me."

5. Noun (*pishechtz* and *pishy*): urine.

> "I won't read this over, because I might not send it and there's not time to write another because it's nearly dawn now what with time out for crying and cursing and once to make *pishy*" (Leslie Fiedler, *The Second Stone*).

PISHER   See *pishen.*

PISHEREL   See *pishen.*

PISHERKEH   See *pishen.*

PISHY   See *pishen.*

PISK

Pronounced "pisk." From the Slavik *pisk*, "jaw."
Noun: a big mouth.

> "John Dean was a *pisk.*"

> The Yiddish saying "Lust has an iron *pisk*" means "Lust consumes everything."

PITSEL

Pronounced "PIT-sell." From the German *Bissel*, "a bit."
Adjective: tiny.

> "Ronald Reagan attended *pitsel* Eureka College."

> "In the end, even Scrooge hoped *pitsel* Tim would live."

PLAGEN

Pronounced "PLOG-en." From the German *plagen*, "to drudge," "to be troubled."
Verb: to work; to suffer.

PLAPLEN

Pronounced "PLAH-plen." From the German *plappern*, "to babble."
Noun: chatter.

PLATKE-MACHER

Also *plotke-macher* and *plyotke-makher*. Pronounced "PLAWD-ke-MA-kher." From the Slavic *platke*, "gossip," and the German *Macher*, "maker."
Noun: a gossip maker.

PLATZ   See *plotz.*

PLOSHER

Pronounced "PLOSH-er." From the German *plaushen*, "to chat."
Noun: a gossip.

PLOTKE-MACHER   See *platke-macher*.

PLOTST   See *plotz*.

PLOTZ

Also *platz* and *plotst*. Pronounced "plots." From the German *platzen*, "to explode."
Verb: to burst; to explode.

> "But what's this about a television? I'm going to get the old lady a new set. I figure I can go for a grand if I have to, and get her a set that will knock her out. I mean that will really spin her head. She'll *plotz* already" (Herbert Selby, Jr., *Requiem for a Dream*).

PLYOTKE-MAKHER   See *platke-macher*.

POTCH   See *patsh*.

POTSH   See *patsh*.

POTSHKEN   See *patshken*.

POTZ   See *putz*.

PRINSESEN

Pronounced "prin-SES-en." From the German *Prinzessin*, "princess."
Noun: a prima donna; a pampered woman.

> "What's a Jewish American *Prinsesen*'s idea of foreplay? (Answer: Three hours of begging.)"

PROST

Pronounced "prahst." Origin unknown.
Adjective: vulgar; low-class.

> "Using salad bowls as skullcaps is pretty *prost*."

PUNIM

Pronounced "POO-nim." From the Hebrew *panim,* "face."
Noun: a face.

"I can't help it that I'm so beautiful they stop Mother when she
is wheeling me in my carriage so as to get a good look at my
gorgeous *punim*—you hear her tell that story, it's something I
myself had nothing to do with, it's a simple fact of nature, that I
was born beautiful and you were born, if not ugly, certainly not
something people wanted to take special looks at" (Philip Roth,
Portnoy's Complaint).

PUPIK

Also *pipik.* Pronounced "PUP-ick." From the Slavic.
1. Noun: a belly button.

On David Frye's record *Richard Nixon Superstar,* Nelson Rocke-
feller assures Nixon that John Lindsay won't be a serious challenge
for the presidency. "I tell you, the people in Queens were going out
of their minds. They were up to their *pupiks* in snow. Elect him?
They wanted to kill him."

A couple of Yiddish expressions are: "He lies with his *pupik* up"
(which means "He's dead") and "He wonders if the flea has a *pupik* "
(meaning he engages in useless speculation).

Mathematicians have a weird sense of humor. In the index to
Joseph Rotman's *The Theory of Groups: An Introduction,* there's an
entry, "Pippik, Moshe. See Navel, Maurice." But under "Navel,
Maurice," you find "See Pippik, Moshe." For some inexplicable
reason, mathematicians often slip jokes into the indexes to their
books. In the index to *Calculus and Analytic Geometry* (by George
B. Thomas, Jr., and Ross L. Finney), which is undoubtedly the most
widely read calculus text in America, there's the curious entry
"Whales." On the page to which the entry directs you there's no
mention of whales. There is, however, a graph that has the shape
of a whale's back.

2. Idiomatic expression: "I've had it up to my *pupik,* " which means "I've
had it up to here."

PUSHKE

Pronounced "PUSH-kuh" or "PUSH-key." From the Polish.

1. Noun: a small box, especially one for collecting money for charity.
2. Noun: a nest egg.

PUSTOPASHNIK   See *pustunpashnik.*

PUSTUNPASHNIK

Also *pustopashnik.* Pronounced "POOST-un-pas-nick." From the Yiddish *pust un pas,* "hollow and idle."
Noun: a loafer.

PUTS   See *putz.*

PUTZ

Also *potz* and *puts.* Pronounced "putts." Perhaps from the German *Putz,* for "ornament" or "adornment." (See the entry for *schmuck* for a discussion of the connection between ornamentation and genitalia.)

1. (Vulgar) noun: penis.

> There is a famous Yiddish folk saying "When the *putz* stands up, the brains get buried in the ground."

> "Look for more kiss-and-tell sports portraits to follow, such as: *The World's Greatest Putts,* by Mrs. Arnold Palmer—'A tale of holey matrimony'" (*The Chicago Reader,* March 5, 1982).

> "Where are you taking me?" Bech asked. His mother replied, "To see something more important than where to put your *putz*" (John Updike, *Bech: A Book*).

2. Noun: a jerk; a "prick."

> "The remedy suggested by the dumb *putz* was limited nuclear war" (Joseph Heller, *Good As Gold*).

> "You're a *putz,*" Gabe Pressman said to his assistant, Barbara Ricks. "You're worse," she said. "I know," Pressman replied (Peter W. Kaplan, "Gabe!," New York *Sunday News Magazine,* October 11, 1981).

"So saith Herr Erwin. Quoth Albert, 'You're nuts. God doesn't play dice with the universe, *putz*' " (Cecil Adams, "The Straight Dope," a poem about the quantum mechanist Erwin Schrödinger, *The Chicago Reader,* May 7, 1982).

"We are in the depths of a depression, Mr. Shimnitz. Are you aware of that? The leaders in the White House don't know their ass from a hot rock how to get us out of it, Mr. Shimnitz. To be blunt about it, Mr. Hoover is a *putz*" (Jerome Weidman, *Tiffany Street*).

3. Verb ("to *putz* around"): to fool around.

"In the American League there's a lot of fussin' and *putzin'* around out there [on the mound]" (Joe Goddard on WGN-AM in Chicago).

RACHMONES
Also *rakhmones.* Pronounced "rahkh-MAW-ness." From the Hebrew *rahmanut,* "compassion."
Noun: compassion; leniency; mercy.

"We all haven't been lucky enough to have been born Jews, you know. So a little *rachmones* on the less fortunate, okay?" (Philip Roth, *Portnoy's Complaint*).

"For your fantastic inability to grasp the implications of the fate of the Fisheries Section in Sovetzki, I should show you the same *rachmones* Trotsky showed the Kronstadt sailors" (Wallace Markfield, *Teitlebaum's Window*).

"*Hab* ['have'] *rachmones,* Lesser, I have my own ambition to realize. I've got fifteen years on you, if not more, and I'm practically naked as the day I was born" (Bernard Malamud, *The Tenants*).

RAKHMONES   See *rachmones.*

REBBE
Pronounced "REB-beh." From the Hebrew *rabi,* "teacher."
Noun: a rabbi.

REBBETSEN   See *rebbitzin.*

REBBITSIN   See *rebbitzin.*

REBBITZIN
Also *rebbetsen* and *rebbitsin.* Pronounced "REB-bit-sin." From the Yiddish *rebbe,* "rabbi."
Noun: the wife of a rabbi.

ROV

Pronounced "rof." From the Hebrew *rav*, "rabbi."
Noun: an ordained rabbi.

Yiddish proverbs link the *rov* to the underworld. For example, "A hometown thief is better than an out-of-town *rov*" and "Treat me like a *rov* and watch me like a thief."

SACHEL

Also *seychel*. Pronounced "SAY-khul." From the Hebrew *sekhel*, "understanding."
Noun: common sense; smarts. Used in such proverbs as "Ask for advice but use your own *sachel*" and "With money you can buy everything except *sachel*."

SAFTIG   See *zaftig*.

SCHATCHEN   See *shadchen*.

SCHLACK   See *schlock*.

SCHLAG

Pronounced "shlahg." From the German *Schlag*, "a blow."
1. Noun: a poor sale.
2. (Box-office slang) noun: a light turnout to buy tickets.

> In Mel Brooks's film *The Producers*, the show *Springtime for Hitler* was designed to be a *schlag*.

SCHLAGER

Pronounced "SHLAHG-er." From the German *Schlag*, "a blow."
Noun: someone who looks like he can be pushed around; a sucker.

> "We closed early that night, I remember, a few minutes before six, though it was a Saturday; and Mr. Z himself chased out the final customer without a pair of shoes. It was unheard of to let a *schlager* walk out without a sale, but as Mr. Z reminded us, 'Christmas comes but once a year' " (Leslie Fiedler, "Nobody Ever Died from It").

SCHLEMASEL   See *schlimazel.*

SCHLEMAZEL   See *schlimazel.*

SCHLEMIEHL   See *schlemiel.*

SCHLEMIEL

Also *schlemiehl, schlemihl, shlemiehl,* and *shlemiel.* Pronounced "shluh-MEEL."

> Origin unknown. Perhaps from the biblical general Shelumiel, whose troops never won a battle. Or perhaps from Shelumiel, a sad sap in the Middle Ages who left his wife for a year, returned home to find a newborn child, and was talked into believing that he had fathered it. The word gained currency in the middle of the nineteenth century because of the popularity of Adelbert von Chamisso's novel *Peter Schlemihl, the Man Without a Shadow.*

Noun: a fool; a blunderbuss; a social misfit who fails because of his own inadequacy. As distinguished from the *schlimazel,* who fails through no fault of his own—just bad luck. (See the discussion under the entry for *schlimazel.*)

> "The fourth was an amiable *schlemiel* who had just about enough sense to sit down when he was tired" (*Saturday Review,* October 6, 1945).

> In Al Capp's cartoon strip "Li'l Abner," a scientist once built a *schlemihlium.*

> "So I said all right, now it's time to eat. But now you're in America, so now you'll eat only American food, so I gave him a banana. Everybody, we all watched, and this *schlemiel,* he never saw a banana before, so naturally, he turns it around in his hands like he's holding something, I don't know, a pistol maybe; he expects it should explode. Go ahead, I said, eat. It's good. It's American food. Eat. So this *schlemiel,* guess what he does? He puts the banana in his mouth, and he starts to eat it, with the skin on it and everything. He eats the whole thing, the skin and all! And all the time, on his face, that stupid smile, like it's good! Like he's enjoying himself!" (Jerome Weidman, *Fourth Street East*).

Jews aren't the only ones who are *schlemiels* when it comes to food. In *The Bell Jar,* Sylvia Plath reports that when she was at Smith College, she received a scholarship donated by a wealthy woman of letters. The woman invited Sylvia to her house for lunch. On the lunch table two finger bowls were placed. Sylvia carefully drank from hers, thinking it was soup. To avoid embarrassing Sylvia, the classy, WASPy hostess started to drink from her own bowl.

SCHLEMIHL   See *schlemiel.*

SCHLEMOZZLE   See *schlimazel.*

SCHLEP

Also *schlepp* and *shlep.* Pronounced "shlep." From the German *schleppen,* "to drag."
1. Verb: to drag.

"Queen Elizabeth will *shlep* along 95 pieces of baggage on her trip here" (*New York Post,* September 19, 1957).

"I know it's summer today. I saw a robin *schlepping* its worm to the beach" (Johnny Carson, the *Tonight* show, June 21, 1979).

Mrs. Rubenstein's husband made a killing in the garment industry. To celebrate, the Rubensteins embarked on a world tour. When they got to Paris, Mrs. Rubenstein went straight to the most expensive boutique on the Champs Élysées. She bought the latest furs, fuzzy hats, lacy support systems, and opera pumps. The stack of purchases reached the upturned nose of the proprietress, who said, "I'll have them sent around to *madame's* hotel."
"*Merci, no!,*" Mrs. Rubenstein replied, thrusting *her* nose into the air. "The hotel's only a block away."
"*Ce n'est pas difficile,*" replied the shopkeeper. "We have a man for just such excursions."
"No problem. *Je* will do it myself," Mrs. Rubenstein said.
"But *madame,*" croaked the proprietress, "why *schlep?*"

2. Verb: to drag one's feet or body around; to walk as if one is dragging heavy packages.

"He *schlepped* home after she kicked him out of her apartment at 2:00 A.M."

" 'The Sheffield' *schlepped* all the way to the Falklands—and for what?"

3. Noun: a slob; a bum. Also *schlepper*.

"And who was to blame? Only myself, I and my fellow *schleps* who, out of sheer magnanimity, had enfranchised women and as thanks been stripped of leadership in the family, the professions and commerce" (S. J. Perelman, "Samson Shorn, or The Slave of Love").

4. Verb: to steal.
5. (Underworld patois) verb: to steal things that have been left in a car.
6. (Underworld patois) noun: the act of stealing things from a car.
7. (Underworld patois) noun (*schlepper*): a car-package thief.
8. (Shoestore slang) noun (*schlepper*): someone who goes from one store to another trying on shoes but never makes a purchase.
9. (Shoestore slang) noun (*schlepper*): a salesman who tries to lure passersby into the store.
10. Noun: someone who is on the lookout for a bargain or a freebie.
11. (Furniture-store jargon) verb: to rearrange the furniture in the store window or on the display floor.

SCHLEPP See *schlep*.

SCHLEPPER See *schlep*.

"IF A SCHLIMAZEL WENT INTO THE HAT BUSINESS, BABIES WOULD BE BORN WITHOUT HEADS."

SCHLIMAZEL

Also *schlemasel, schlemazel, shlemozzle, shlimazel,* and *shlimazl.* Pronounced "shli-MAH-zel." From the German *schlimm,* "bad," and the Hebrew *mazal,* "luck."
1. Noun: a born loser; someone who's always unlucky.

> The *schlimazel* is the subject of many Yiddish proverbs. "When a *schlimazel* falls on his back, he breaks his nose." "When a *schlimazel* winds a clock, it stops." "When a *schlimazel* kills a rooster, it continues to hop." "If a *schlimazel* sold candles, the sun would never set." "If a *schlimazel* went into the hat business, babies would be born without heads."
>
> The *schlemiel* brings on his own misfortune, unlike the *schlimazel* who gets it handed to him. For example, when a *schlimazel* drops a piece of buttered toast, it always lands buttered side down. But when a *schlemiel* drops a piece of toast, he has buttered both sides. (The *nebbish* is the one who cleans up the mess.)

2. Noun (*chimozzle, schlemozzle, shemozzle, shimozzle,* and *shlemozzle*): confusion; a complication; a mess. Chiefly Canadian and British.

> "Those . . . who saw so little of war that they still think of it to be a gloriously romantic *shlemozzle*" (*Sunday Dispatch,* July 29, 1928).

3. Verb (*shemozzle*): to run away from a mess. Chiefly Canadian and British.

SCHLOCK

Also *schlack, shlak,* and *shlock.* Origin unknown. Perhaps from the German *Schlag,* "a blow"; *schlocky* goods being beat-up goods.
1. Noun or adjective: something shoddy; poorly crafted. (The adjective form is *schlocky* as well as *schlock.*)

> "Critics charge that affordable art is '*schlock*' and that people are buying it instead of 'legitimate art'" (William E. Geist, "A Picture Over the Sofa," *The New York Times,* December 1, 1981).

> "The label 'Made in Japan' used to mean *schlock* but now it means quality" (*The New York Times,* July 23, 1982).

2. Noun: a peeve; a complainer; a wretch.
3. (Furniture-store slang) noun: an overcharge.

SCHLOCK

4. Noun (*shlock house* or *shlock joint*): a store that sells inferior merchandise.
5. (Furniture-store slang) noun (*shlock joint*): a store without fixed prices.
6. Noun (*schlock meister*): someone who specializes in selling cheap merchandise. Literally, "a master of *schlock*."

> "The word [preppy] was more or less invented in 1970 by Erich Segal in *Love Story*, the novel in which Segal also popularized the phrase, 'Love is not having to call me a *schlock meister*' " (Calvin Trillin, *The Nation*, February 7, 1981). The implication is that Segal, a professor of classics, is a *schlock meister* for turning out *Love Story*.

7. Noun (*schlock minister*): a preacher who solicits contributions over the radio.

SCHLOCK MEISTER   See *schlock*.

SCHLOCK MINISTER   See *schlock*.

SCHLOCKY   See *schlock*.

SCHLOOMP   See *shlump*.

SCHLUMP   See *shlump.*

SCHM-   See *shm-*

SCHMAHLTS   See *schmaltz.*

SCHMALTZ
Also *schmahlts, shmahlts, shmaltz,* and *shmawlts.* Pronounced "shmahlts."
From the German *Schmalz,* "melted fat" or "grease."
1. Noun: melted fat, especially chicken fat.

> "Some connoisseurs of Jewish cooking claim . . . that the *schmaltz* [is] thicker at Sammy's" (*The New York Times,* August 21, 1981).

> "Why must someone who is trying to enjoy a simple plate of chopped liver be interrupted constantly by pure-food fanatics, one of whom is almost certainly his own wife, telling him that he is downing the equivalent of ground glass with *schmaltz*?" (Calvin Trillin, *The Nation,* June 28, 1980).

2. Noun: mawkishness; oversentimentality; pathos.

> "Turn off that *schmaltz,*" said convicted murderess Barbara Graham (played by Susan Hayward), referring to the music pumped into the death house the morning before she was executed (in the movie *I Want to Live*).

> "But after she had gone on a while, he would say, 'Enough enough of this Weimar *schmaltz.* Cut it, Margotte!' That big virile interruption would never be heard again in this cockeyed living room" (Saul Bellow, *Mr. Sammler's Planet*).

3. Verb ("to *schmaltz* up"): to make maudlin.
4. Noun: hair tonic.

> "I used olive oil for *schmaltz.* But chicken fat is still the best *schmaltz*" (T. Betts, *Across the Board,* 1956).

5. (Army and navy slang) noun (*schmaltz artist*): a sycophant.
6. Adjective (*schmaltzy*): too sentimental, mushy, corny, or gaudy.

> " 'You become a walking Pulitzer and so, even when you croak the first words of the obituary are "Pulitzer prizewinner passes." '

He had a point, I thought. 'And Charlie is a double Pulitzer. First came that *schmaltzy* play. Which made him a fortune on Broadway. Plus movie rights. He got a percentage of the gross' " (Saul Bellow, *Humboldt's Gift*).

SCHMALTZY   See *schmaltz.*

SCHMATE

Also *schmatta, schmattah, shmata, shmate, shmatte,* and *shmotte.* Pronounced "SHMAH-tah." From the Polish *szmata,* "rag."
1. Noun: a rag; a cheap dress; a shoddy garment.

"You can't hardly rummage through your own *schmottas* nowadays without some ignatz snaps your head off" (S. J. Perelman, "Zwei Herzen in die Drygoods Schlock").

"She had on a tired old *schmattah* and I was wearing an expensive knitted pants suit" (Xaviera Hollander, *Xaviera!*).

If you listen closely to the song "Shattered" on the Rolling Stones' album *Some Girls,* you can hear *schmate* three times.

On the *Dick Van Dyke Show* there was a Japanese designer called Mr. *Schmate.*

2. Noun: anything that is cheap or worthless.
3. Noun: a slut.

SCHMATTA   See *schmate.*

SCHMATTAH   See *schmate.*

SCHMEAR   See *shmeer.*

SCHMECK   See *shmeck.*

SCHMEER   See *shmeer.*

SCHMEISS   See *shmeis.*

SCHMIER   See *shmeer.*

SCHMISS   See *shmeis.*

SCHMO   See *shmo.*

SCHMOCK   See *schmuck.*

SCHMOE   See *shmo.*

SCHMUCK

Also *schmock, shmock,* and *shmuck.* Pronounced "shmuck." From the
German *Schmuck,* "ornament," "decoration," or "jewelry."
1. (Vulgar) noun: penis

> In English the connection between ornamentation and genitalia
> can be found in the cute euphemism "family jewels," and in one of
> Vladimir Nabokov's many colorful expressions for the male mem-
> ber, "scepter of passion." In Yiddish the connection is more obscene.
> Example: "In her dreams there were no holes barred to his *schmuck.*"

2. (Vulgar) noun: an idiot; a fool.

> New York Mayor Ed Koch once posed for photographers at the
> Pyramids by donning Arab headgear and sitting between the mangy
> humps of a camel named "California," yet back in the States he
> refused to mug with a rare white Bengal tiger. Said Koch: "No, the
> Mayor is not a coward and the Mayor is also not a *schmuck*!" ("The
> Man Behind the Mayor," *The New York Times Magazine,* February
> 1, 1981).

> "The same Maddox report said, 'The simple folksy manner of
> John Wayne can be effective with the target group.' And that, Kevin
> Phillips said, was an insight. 'Wayne might sound bad to people in
> New York, but he sounds great to the *schmucks* we're trying to
> reach through John Wayne. The people down there in the Yahoo
> belt' " (Joe McGinniss, *The Selling of the President 1968*).

> "Unfortunately, Satan gets a psychiatrist, Dr. Seymour Kassler,
> J.S.P.S. (Just Some Poor *Schmuck*), who is in even worse shape"
> (review of Jeremy Levin's *Satan: His Psychotherapy and Cure by the
> Unfortunate Dr. Kassler* in *The New York Times Book Review*).

3. (Vulgar) noun: a bastard, a son of a bitch.

"It costs a lot to carve *schmuck* on a tombstone, but in your case it would be worth it" (Lee Remick in the movie *The Competition*).

SCHNAPS   See *shnaps*.

SCHNECK

Perhaps from the German *Schnake*, "lighthearted nonsense."
1. Noun: affectation.
2. Noun: sexual advances, particularly ones not backed up by feeling.

"The arm of the specially-invited young man was round her as she spoke. 'Don't make *Schnecks*,' said Fanny" (Israel Zangwill, *Children of the Ghetto*, 1892).

SCHNECKEN

Also *shnecken*. Pronounced "SHNECK-en."
Noun: little fruitcakes or nut cakes.

"When I first met Freud, I was already at work on my theories. Freud was in a bakery. He was attempting to buy some *Schnecken*, but could not bear to ask for them by name. Freud was too embarrassed to say the word '*Schnecken*,' as you probably know. 'Let me have some of those little cakes,' he would say, pointing to them.

"The baker said, 'You mean these *Schnecken*, Herr Professor?'

"At that, Freud flushed crimson and fled out the door muttering, 'Er, no–nothing–never mind' " (Woody Allen, *Getting Even*).

SCHNEIDER

Also *shnayder*. Pronounced "SHNY-der." From the German *Schneider*, "tailor."
1. Noun: a tailor.

The *schneider* was upset about the way business was going. "Goldie," he said to his wife, "the only way I could do well is if the Messiah helped me."

"How could the Messiah help you? " she asked.

"Well," replied the *schneider*, "he could bring back the dead."

"How would that help?" she asked.

"They would need clothes," he answered.

"But there are other tailors among the dead," Goldie shrewdly countered.

"Ah yes. But they don't know the latest fashions."

"To her the old Jewish words for these trades—*Schneider, Schuster* [shoemaker]—were terms of contempt" (Saul Bellow, "The Old People").

2. (Garment-worker slang) noun: anyone connected with the garment industry.
3. Verb: to win a game, especially gin rummy, before the opponent is able to score even a single point.
4. Noun: a shutout, as in baseball or gin rummy.

SCHNOOK   See *shnook*.

SCHNORRER

Also *shnorrer*. Pronounced "shnorer." From the German *schnorren*, "to beg." Perhaps the German word is onomatopoeic for the sound of the musical horns once played by strolling beggars.
1. Noun: a beggar; a panhandler.

"My first hello in Rome and it has to be a *schnorrer*" (Bernard Malamud, "The Last Mohican").

"The crowd of half-starved immigrants, consisting of street hawkers and *schnorrers*, who are the plague of the Jewish Board of Guardians" (*Daily Chronicle*, March 10, 1899).

"He did not foresee the day when, a *schnorrer* indeed, he would have taken five shillings from anybody who could afford it . . ." (Israel Zangwill, *Dreamers of the Ghetto*, 1898).

In the Marx Brothers' film *Animal Crackers*, the chorus sings, "Hooray for Captain Spaulding, the African explorer." Groucho promptly asks, "Did someone call me *schnorrer*?"

The definition of forty-three across in the crossword puzzle in the August 15, 1982, issue of *The New York Times Magazine* was "picnic *schnorrer*." The answer was "ant."

In *Fiddler on the Roof,* a *schnorrer,* who has heard a rich man complain about his economic hardships, says, "So if you had a bad week, why should I suffer?"

2. Verb (to *schnor*): to beg.

" 'But isn't it *schnorring* to be dependent on strangers?' inquired Esther with bitter amusement" (Israel Zangwill, *Children of the Ghetto,* 1892).

3. Noun: a cheapskate; a miser.

4. (Shoestore slang) noun: a customer who haggles in a store where the prices are fixed.

SCHNOZZ   See *shnoz.*

SCHNOZZLE   See *shnoz.*

SCHNOZZLER   See *shnoz.*

SCHNOZZO   See *shnoz.*

SCHNOZZOLA   See *shnoz.*

SCHREIEN
Pronounced "SHRY-en." From the German *schreien,* "to cry out." Verb: to complain or talk loudly.

SCHTETL   See *shtetl.*

SCHTICK   See *shtik.*

SCHTIK   See *shtik.*

SCHTUP   See *shtup.*

SCHVARTZ
Pronounced "shvartz." From the German *schwarz,* "black."
1. Adjective: black.

Some typical Yiddish sayings are: "If the chimney sweep fights with the miller, the chimney sweep will turn white and the miller *schvartz* " and "All cows are *schvartz* at night."

2. Noun (*schvartze* or *schvartzeh* for a female; *schvartzer* for a man): a black person. Usually refers to domestics.

"She sews, she knits, she darns—she irons better even than the *schvartze*, to whom, of all her friends who each possess of this grinning childish black old lady's hide, she alone is good" (Philip Roth, *Goodbye Columbus*).

"How many Jews does it take to screw in a lightbulb? (Answer: Three—one to call the *schvartze* and two to feel guilty about calling her.)" (Matt Freedman and Paul Hoffman, *How Many Zen Buddhists Does It Take to Screw in a Lightbulb?*)

In the Mel Brooks film *Blazing Saddles,* an Indian chief and his braves surround a terrified black man and his family. "They're darker than us!" exclaims the chief. He calls one of his braves over for counsel. "Ah . . . ma . . . ma . . . yah . . . vah . . . *shvartzes?*" he asks.

SCHVARTZE   See *schvartz.*

SCHVARTZEH   See *schvartz.*

SCHVARTZER   See *schvartz.*

SCHWANZ   See *shvontz.*

SCHWINDLE   See *shvindle.*

SEYCHEL   See *sachel.*

SHABBES

Also *shabes.* Pronounced "SHAH-bus." From the Hebrew *shabbat,* "rest." Noun: the Sabbath.

"In time I was going to explain to you why Trotsky didn't come back for Lenin's funeral from Sukham in the Caucasus and how a whole generation of Soviet experts has displayed such fantastic ignorance of the fact that the funeral was on a Saturday and in a million years and for all the Russias Trotsky would not ride on *Shabbes*" (Wallace Markfield, *Teitlebaum's Window*).

"Our beloved rabbi is so holy," boasted a man from Minsk, "that when he goes out walking in the rain, everywhere else it is raining, but where he steps, it is not raining."

"So?" said a man from Chelm. "Our rabbi is so holy that when he rides a horse on *Shabbes,* everywhere else it is *Shabbes,* but where he is riding, it is not *Shabbes.*"

SHABBES GOY

Pronounced "SHAH-bus goy." From the Yiddish *Shabbes,* "Sabbath," and *goy,* "a gentile male."

1. Noun: a non-Jew hired by Orthodox Jews to turn lights on and off and to perform other physical tasks that Jews are forbidden to do on the Sabbath.

> " 'There he goes,' they would say on Saturday mornings, as my father set out on the long walk to Lafayette Street. 'The neighborhood *Shabbes goy* ' " (Jerome Weidman, *Fourth Street East*).

2. Noun: a disparaging term for a Jew who strays from the faith.

SHABES   See *shabbes.*

SHADCHAN   See *shadchen.*

SHADCHEN

Also *schatchen, shadchan,* and *shadkhen.* Pronounced "SHODD-khen." From the Hebrew *shadkhan,* "marriage broker."
Noun: a marriage broker; a matchmaker.

> "Without delay, he made inquiries about the fair young vision, and, finding its respectability unimpeachable, he sent a *shadchen* to propose to her, and they were affianced" (Israel Zangwill, *Children of the Ghetto,* 1892).

> In the parking lot behind the temple, the *shadchen* introduced Shlomo to the girl she had in mind for him. Shlomo was horrified. He pulled the *shadchen* aside and whispered, "How can you fix me up with such a creature? She's inept in conversation, ugly as sin, and blind as a bat."
> "You don't need to whisper," replied the *shadchen.* "She's deaf, too."

In *Jokes and Their Relation to the Unconscious,* Sigmund Freud analyzed several jokes that involve *shadchens.* The following joke succeeds, Freud wrote, because it takes pains to string together a series of sophistical statements in order to create the appearance of a coherent, logical argument: The *Schadchen* was defending the girl he had proposed against the young man's protests. "I don't care for the mother-in-law," said the latter. "She's a disagreeable, stupid person."—"But after all you're not marrying the mother-in-law. What you want is her daughter."—"Yes, but she's not young any longer, and she's not precisely a beauty."—"No matter. If she's neither young nor beautiful she'll be all the more faithful to you." —"And she hasn't much money."—"Who's talking about money? Are you marrying money then? After all it's a wife that you want." —"But she's got a hunchback too."—"Well, what *do* you want? Isn't she to have a single fault?"

The success of the next joke Freud also attributed to thinly disguised sophistry: The would-be bridegroom complained that the bride had one leg shorter than the other and limped. The *Schadchen* contradicted him: "You're wrong. Suppose you marry a woman with healthy straight limbs! What do you gain from it? You never have a day's security that she won't fall down, break a leg and afterwards be lame all her life. And think of the suffering then, the agitation, and the doctor's bill! But if you take *this* one, that can't happen to you. Here you have a *fait accompli.*"

The next joke owes its humorous punch, Freud said, to a double meaning: The *Schadchen* had assured the suitor that the girl's father was no longer living. After the betrothal it emerged that the father was still alive and was serving a prison sentence. The suitor protested to the *Schadchen,* who replied: "Well, what did I tell you? You surely don't call that living?"

The last joke succeeds because it is funny when someone gets so carried away in making a point that he slips up: The bridegroom was paying his first visit to the bride's house in the company of the *Schadchen,* and while they were waiting in the *salon* for the family to appear, the marriage broker drew attention to a cupboard with glass doors in which the finest set of silver plate was exhibited. "There! Look at that! You can see from these things how rich these people are."—"But," asked the suspicious young man, "mightn't it be possible that these fine things were only collected for the occasion

—that they were borrowed to give an impression of wealth?"—
"What an idea!" answered the *Schadchen* protestingly. "Who do
you think would lend these people anything?"

SHADKHEN See *shadchen*.

SHAH

Pronounced like the one in Iran, but faster.
Exclamation: Hush! Shut up!

"'*Shah*!' she shouts, turning her head to glare angrily in the
direction of these noisy late-comers [in the theater]. The word '*shah*'
is like the word 'fire'; nothing spreads more quickly" (Ethel Rosenberg, "Mrs. Rivkin Grapples with the Drama").

SHAINKEIT

Pronounced "SHAYN-kite." From the German *schön*, "beautiful."
Noun: beauty.

"*Shainkeit* is only skin-deep, but ugliness goes straight to the
bone."

In Woody Allen's movie *Love and Death*, a *shainkeit* whispers to
him, "My room at midnight."
"Great!" Allen replies. "Will you be there, too?"

SHALOM

Also *sholem* and *shol'm*. Pronounced "SHAH-lohm." From the Hebrew
shalom, "peace."
1. Noun: peace.
2. Salutation: hello or good-bye. Yiddish has the greeting *shalom aleichem*,
"peace be with you," and the obligatory response *aleichem shalom*, "and
peace to you."

Sholem Aleichem was the nom de plume of the Russian-born
humorist Solomon Rabinowitz (1859–1916).

"Well, the Hebrew word for hello is *shalom*. . . . And the word
for good-bye is *shalom*," said a presidential aide (played by Georgie
Jessel) prior to a visit by Golda Meir.
"How do I tell which is which?" the President asked.

"If she leaves after you've said it," replied the aide, "you've said good-bye" (from David Frye's record *I Am the President*).

SHAMES   See *shamus.*

SHAMMUS   See *shamus.*

SHAMOS   See *shamus.*

SHAMUS

Also *shames, shammus, shamos,* and *shommes.* Pronounced "SHAH-mis" (for a guard) and "SHAY-mis" (for a policeman). From the Hebrew *shamas,* "caretaker of a synagogue."
1. Noun: a guard, detective, or policeman.

> "Not a real copper at that. Just a cheap *shamus"* (Raymond Chandler, "Farewell, My Lovely," 1940).

2. Noun: a police informer.
3. Noun: anyone who sucks up to a politician.

> Harold Wentworth, in *The Dictionary of American Slang,* suggests that this meaning may have been influenced by the Irish proper name "Shamus," although he notes that the American Indian word *shamon,* "medicine man," also has the slang meaning of "sycophant."

SHANDA

Also *shande* and *shonda.* Pronounced "SHAWN-duh."
Noun: shame; an embarrassment; a scandal.

> "You're a *shonda* to your race" (Joseph Heller, *Good As Gold*).
> In *Fiddler on the Roof* Tevye, the dairyman—played by Zero Mostel—utters the famous Yiddish adage "Poverty is no *shanda,* but it's no great honor either."

SHANDE   See *shanda.*

SHANDHOIZ

Pronounced "SHAWND-hoyce." From the Yiddish *shanda,* "shame," and *hoiz,* "house." Literally, "house of shame."
Noun: a house of prostitution.

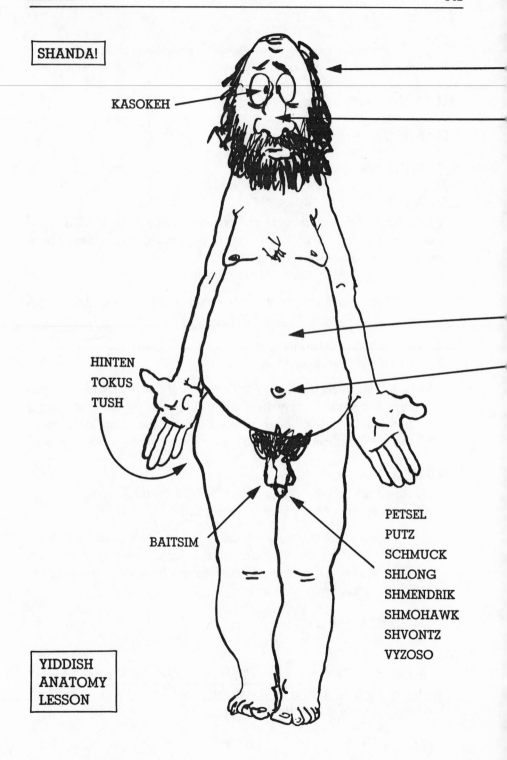

SHANDA!

KASOKEH

HINTEN
TOKUS
TUSH

BAITSIM

PETSEL
PUTZ
SCHMUCK
SHLONG
SHMENDRIK
SHMOHAWK
SHVONTZ
VYZOSO

YIDDISH
ANATOMY
LESSON

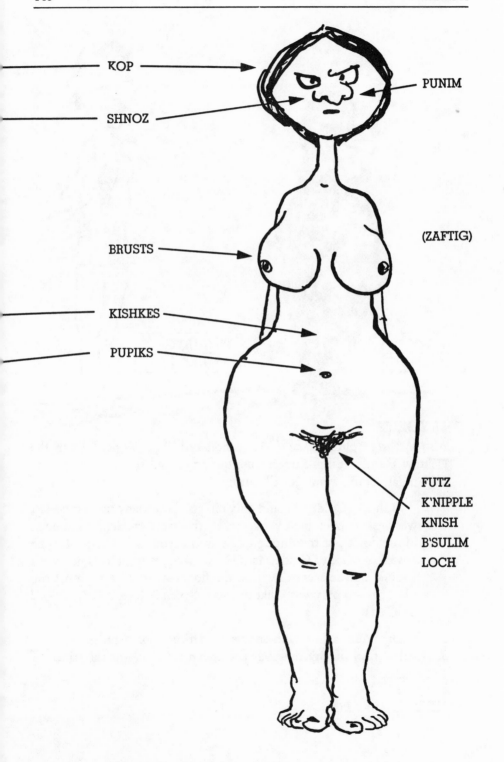

KOP

PUNIM

SHNOZ

(ZAFTIG)

BRUSTS

KISHKES

PUPIKS

FUTZ
K'NIPPLE
KNISH
B'SULIM
LOCH

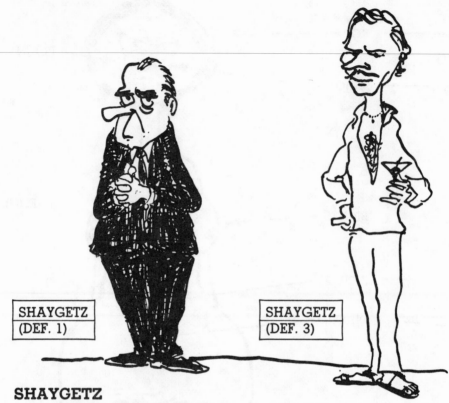

SHAYGETZ
(DEF. 1)

SHAYGETZ
(DEF. 3)

SHAYGETZ

Also *sheygetz* (plural: *shkutsim*). Pronounced "SHAY-gits." From the Hebrew *shekets*, "disgusting because uncircumcised."

1. (Vulgar) noun: a non-Jewish male.

> "Oh, Dr. Gold, if I could only tell you how many times my heart was broken, over and over again, by that *momzer* Henry Kissinger. Please don't put me through that again. How sick I was when he raised his voice to Golda Meir. How I wept, wept, Dr. Gold, when I found out he went down on the floor—without even a hat on, I betcha—to pray with that *shaygetz* Nixon" (Joseph Heller, *Good As Gold*).

2. (Vulgar) noun: a Jew who adopts the attitudes of gentiles.
3. Noun: a man of any religious persuasion who charms the pants off women.

SHEENIE See *sheeny.*

SHEENY
Also *sheenie.* Pronounced "SHE-nee." Perhaps from the German *schön,* "pretty," or from the Yiddish *miesse meshina,* "an ugly death." May also be related to the German *Schin,* "a low-class thief."
(Vulgar) noun: a Jew.

The Jews have developed clever retorts to slurs such as *sheeny* and other anti-Semitic utterances. Example: "Israel Zangwill, the British-Jewish writer, once found himself at a fancy dinner party, seated next to a well-dressed matron. Zangwill was tired and without thinking, he yawned—right in the face of the woman beside him. Taken aback by this rude behavior, she said to him, 'Please mind your Jewish manners. I was afraid you were going to swallow me.' 'Have no fear, madam,' Zangwill replied. 'My religion prohibits my doing that'" (William Novak and Moshe Waldoks, *The Big Book of Jewish Humor*).

SHEKEL
Pronounced "SHECK-cull." From the Hebrew *shequel,* "weight" or "coin" (a silver coin in ancient Babylonia that weighed about two thirds of an ounce).
1. Noun: a coin, especially a silver dollar. (Today the *shekel* is also a unit of currency in Israel.)

"In America the streets are lined with golden *shekels.*"

2. Noun: weight.

SHEMOZZLE   See *schlimazel.*

SHEYGETZ   See *shaygetz.*

SHICK   See *shikker.*

SHICKER   See *shikker.*

SHICKERED   See *shikker.*

SHICKERY   See *shikker.*

SHICKSA See *shiksa*.

SHIHI-PIHI

Pronounced "SHE-he-PEE-he." Perhaps from the two kinds of bodily wastes.
Noun: a mere bagatelle; nothing.

" '*Shihi-pihi*!,' she exclaimed as she rifled through his drawers."

SHIKER See *shikker*.

SHIKKER

Also *shicker* and *shiker*. Pronounced "SHICK-er." From the Hebrew *shikor*, "drunkard."
1. Noun: a drunkard.

> Shlomo was quite distressed because he didn't know how his son was going to earn a living. He went to consult his rabbi. "I know how you can find out," the rabbi told him. "This evening put out on the table a jug of wine, a bible, and a wad of money. Hide in the next room and see which object your son takes. If he chooses the wine, it means he's going to become a *shikker*. If he takes the *gelt*, it means he'll make a lot of money, like you. And if he picks the bible, he'll become a holy man, like me."
> Shlomo went home, put out the three objects, and hid in the next room. His son appeared. He promptly drank the wine, stuffed the money in his pocket, pressed the bible to his breast, and left the house.
> Shlomo was flabbergasted. He immediately called up the rabbi. "What does this mean?," he asked.
> "Oh, my God!," the rabbi exclaimed. "He's going to become a Roman Catholic priest."

> "He's a good boy—you don't have to worry. He won't be a *shicker* or a wife-beater, God forbid, but a scholar he'll never be, if you know what I mean, although maybe a good mechanic. It's no disgrace in these times" (Bernard Malamud, "The Jewbird").

> "You Jews have funny ideas about drinking. Especially the one that all Gentiles are born drunkards. You have a song about it—

'Drunk he is, drink he must, because he is a *Goy* . . . *Schicker*' " (Saul Bellow, *The Victim*).

2. Adjective (*shick, shickered,* and *shickery*): a drunk. A common Australian colloquialism.

"I'm always that fresh after a good night's sleep, when I've had a bit of a spree that I could begin again quite flippant. Old Tom had a goodish cheque this time, and was at it a week afore I came in. He was rayther *shickery*" (Rolf Boldrenwood, *An Australian Squire,* 1878).

"They sat outside the pub in the sun every day, and most of them got a bit *shickered* on pension day" (Gavin Casey, *Downhill Is Easier,* 1945).

3. Adjective ("on the *shicker*"): drinking. Australian idiom.

"One night the magician had been on the *shicker,* and with a fine disregard for life and limb he let the lion out" (Roy Rene, *Mo's Memoirs,* 1945).

4. Verb: to get drunk. Australian colloquialism.
5. Noun: liquor. Australian colloquialism.

SHIKSA

Also *shicksa, shikse,* and *shikseh.* Pronounced "SHICK-suh." From the Hebrew *sheques,* "blemish."

1. Noun: a non-Jewish woman, especially one who is young and attractive.

"What do you think of that, Stingo? Here I am pushing thirty years old. I fall crazy in love with a Polish *shiksa* and she keeps her sweet treasure all locked up as tightly as little Shirley Mirmelstein I tried to make out with for five whole years" (William Styron, *Sophie's Choice*).

"The burden of the plot is borne by Richard's pathetic affair with Wimsy, a vapid little '*shiksa*' with a perpetual cold in the nose and a habit of responding to all crises with 'a sharp whimper,' 'a little cry,' and 'an excited giggle' " (Wallace Markfield's review of *Remember Me to God* by Myron S. Kaufmann, *Commentary*, November 1957).

"Benny marry a *shiksa*? It can't be! Ah well, like so many other things in life that can't be, it is" (Jerome Weidman, *Tiffany Street*).

In the movie *Sleeper*, Diane Keaton imitates Woody Allen's mother. Keaton says, "Be quiet and eat your *shiksa*."

"Mister Touch-Me-Not," she said, "so ashamed of his mother he wants his blue-eyed *shikses* to think he came out from a rock, I suppose" (John Updike, *Bech: A Book*).

2. Noun: a Jewish woman who strays from the faith.

SHIKSE   See *shiksa*.

SHIKSEH   See *shiksa*.

SHIMOZZLE   See *schlimazel*.

SHKUTSIM   See *shaygetz*.

SHLAK   See *schlock*.

SHLANG   See *shlong*.

SHLECT
Rhymes with "decked." From the German *schlecht*, "bad."
Adjective: bad.

"The thief has an easy job but *shlect* dreams" is a Yiddish proverb.

SHLEMIEHL   See *schlemiel*.

SHLEMIEL   See *schlemiel*.

SHLEMOZZLE   See *schlimazel*.

SHLEP   See *schlep.*

SHLIMAZEL   See *schlimazel.*

SHLIMAZL   See *schlimazel.*

SHLOCK   See *schlock.*

SHLOGEN
Pronounced "SHLOG-en." From the German *schlagen,* "to beat."
Verb: to beat up.

SHLONG
Also *shlang.* Pronounced "shlong." From the German *Schlange,* "snake"
or "coil."
1. Noun: penis

> "Boomie murmured, '*Oy oy oy,* mine Marshell*eh* god hah *shlong*
> like King Kong'" (Wallace Markfield, *Teitlebaum's Window*).

> On the way to a party given by New York Mayor John Lindsay,
> Alexander Portnoy tries to restrain Mary Jane Reed's vulgarity by
> telling her, "Don't make a grab for Big John's *shlong* until we've been
> there at least half an hour, okay?" (Philip Roth, *Portnoy's Complaint*).

> The movie *Last Tango in Paris* contains this snippet of bedroom
> conversation:
> Marlon Brando: "Hap-penis."
> Marie Schneider: "Hap-penis?"
> Brando: *"Shlong!"*

2. Noun: a troublesome wife.

> "His *shlong* was very uncooperative in bed."

SHLOOMP   See *shlump.*

SHLOSSER
Pronounced "shlaucer." From the German.
Noun: mechanic.

> "Mr. Goodwrench is a *shlosser.*"

SHLUB See *zhlub.*

SHLUBBO See *zhlub.*

SHLUHB See *zhlub.*

SHLUMP
Also *schloomp, schlump,* and *shloomp.* Pronounced "shloomp." From the German *Schlumpe,* "slovenly female" or "slut."
1. Noun: a slob; a drip.
2. Verb: to droop.
3. Verb: to do something in a half-assed and unenthusiastic way.

"YOUR MOTHER'S SUCH A SHLUMPER
SHE SWIMS OUT TO MEET TROOPSHIPS"

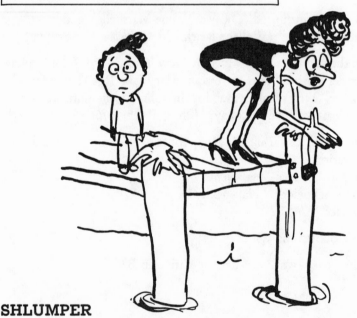

SHLUMPER
Pronounced "SHLOOMP-er." From the German *Schlumpe,* "slut."
Noun: a slut.

"Your mother's such a *shlumper* she swims out to meet troopships."

SHLUMPERDIK

Also *shlumpy*. Pronounced "SHLOOMP-er-dick." From the Yiddish *shlump*, "slob."
Adjective: sloppy; unkempt.

"And moving the clothes was that walk that was not a walk, the tiny-stepped *shlumpy* gait" (Philip Roth, "Eli, the Fanatic").

SHLUMPY   See *shlumperdik.*

SHM-

Also *schm-*. This is a deprecating prefix, and it is found in numerous words (*schmatte, schmuck, shmegegge, shmendrik, shmo,* and so on).

The prefix *shm-* can serve to pooh-pooh any word if the word is first stated and then repeated with *shm-* in place of the initial consonant(s). For example, *fancy-shmancy, wife-shmife, Freud-Shmeud, Oedipus-Shmoedipus* ("as long as he loves his mother"), *Cancer-Shmancer,* ("as long as she's healthy"), and *Dictionary-Shmictionary!*

"*Love-shmuv.* What does a young boy or girl know about what is good for them?" (Isaac Bashevis Singer, "The Needle").

"His hands shot down to cover his crotch. Goldie looked at him, mystified, while Epstein searched for words appropriate to his posture. At last! 'You had a nice bath?' '*Nice, shmice,* it was a bath' " (Philip Roth, "Epstein").

During the student uprisings of the 1960's, *The Wall Street Journal* carried the headline "*REVOLUTION, SHMEVOLUTION.*"

A full-page ad for *Fortune* magazine in the January 28, 1981, issue of *The New York Times* began "*Loyalty, Shmoyalty.*"

In 1950 *The Daily Herald* ran an article about infighting in the philosophy department of Vassar College. The headline was "*Plato-Shmato.*"

In *Lolita* Vladimir Nabokov resorts to some rich wordplay when he has Claire Quilty say, "I have been called the American Maeterlinck. *Maeterlinck-Schmetterling,* says I." Maeterlinck was an Austrian playwright who won a Nobel Prize, and *Schmetterling* is the German word for "butterfly." Nabokov himself was an avid butterfly collector.

"*Consommé schmonsommé,*" says a character in the movie *Bowery Battalion.*

In the cartoon strip "Phoebe & the Pigeon People" in the May 7, 1982, *Chicago Reader,* an old man says, "*Fabric, Schmabric!* That plastic slip–cover that's *on* the couch cost me $69.95!"

The same deprecating effect can be achieved by reversing the word order. An advertisement in the November/December 1981 issue of *Games* magazine read: "Heads or tails? Either way, shmuzzling can only be accomplished with the original *Shmuzzle Puzzle,* the puzzle which fits together trillions of ways only one of which is correct."

"Naa!" Zucky urged. "*Schreck-dreck* by de daw—he's de best spider in de woild" (Henry Roth, *Call It Sleep*).

SHMACK   See *shmeck.*

SHMAHLTS   See *schmaltz.*

SHMALTZ   See *schmaltz.*

SHMATA   See *schmate.*

SHMATE   See *schmate.*

SHMATTE   See *schmate.*

SHMAWLTS   See *schmaltz.*

SHMEAR   See *shmeer.*

SHMECK

Also *schmeck.* Not from the German *schmecken,* "to taste."
1. Noun: smell.

2. (Underworld patois) noun: narcotics, especially powdered drugs.
3. (Underworld patois) noun (also *shmack*): heroin; "smack."
4. (Underworld patois) noun (*shmecker*): drug user.

SHMECKER   See *shmeck*.

SHMEER (DEF. 3)

SHMEER (DEF. 2)

SHMEER (DEF. 6)

SHMEER

Also *schmear*, *schmeer*, *schmier*, and *shmear*. Pronounced "shmeer." From the German *schmieren*, "to grease."
1. Verb: to smear.

> "While you stand here *schmiering* on canvas, over there is a wizard creating miracles" (S. J. Perelman, "Methinks the Lady Doth Propel Too Much").

2. (Delicatessen slang) noun: a glob of cream cheese.

> "Do you want a bagel with a *shmeer*?"

3. Verb: to grease the palm of; to bribe.

> "Harrison Williams was *shmeered*."

4. Noun: a bribe
5. Noun: everything; the whole deal; the shebang.

> "When you buy the beer-making kit, you get the whole *shmeer* —the brewing vessel, the hops, the bottles and the caps," said the owner of a wine- and beer-making store in Boston.

6. (Sports jargon) verb: to wipe out an opponent.

> "Brandeis *shmeered* Holy Cross."

7. (Furniture-store slang) verb: to flatter a customer.

SHMEGEGGE

Also *shmegeggi* and *shmigegge*. Pronounced so as to end with "eggy."

> Lillian Mermin Feinsilver, author of *The Taste of Yiddish*, thinks *shmegegge* may be a combination of two other Yiddish words for "fool," the obscene *schmuck* and *yeke* (a disparaging word for a German Jew that has come to mean someone who is arrogant and foolish).

Noun: a buffoon; an idiot.

> "And so you laugh boisterously, feeling not a little superior to the poor *shmigegge*, while all the time it is you who are the target!" (Nathan Ausubel, *A Treasury of Jewish Humor*).

SHMEGEGGI See *shmegegge*.

SHMEIKLE

Pronounced "SHMY-cull."
Verb: to talk someone into something.

SHMEIS

Also *schmeiss* and *schmiss*. Pronounced "shmice." From the German *schmeissen*, "to hurl" or "to slam."
1. Noun: bang.

> " 'Young man,' he said, smiling and tapping a finger against the lacquered board [on which they were playing craps], 'you have a friend here.' He pointed at himself. 'You understand? You have a

friend here. Go ahead. *Schmeiss*!' His hand struck the counter with a light, slapping sound" (Chaim Potok, *The Promise*).

2. (Furniture-store slang): to break off a sale, especially because the store offers such bad terms that the customer walks out. Example: "The sale was *shmeised*."

SHMENDRICK   See *shmendrik*.

SHMENDRIK

Also *shmendrick*. Pronounced "SHMEN-drick." Origin unclear. Perhaps a derogatory form of the name "Hendrik," a character in an operetta by Abraham Goldfaden.
1. Noun: a weak, ineffectual person.

In the movie *Robin and the Seven Hoods,* the hoods decide to picket Robin, played by Frank Sinatra. One of them carries a sign that reads, "Robin Is a *Shmendrik.*"

2. Noun: little penis. Used by women as an affectionate put-down.

" '*Shmendrick!*' she said. 'Big Brother is watching. Do you call this croquet?' She had not called him *shmendrick,* Howard realized, since they were both fifteen and they had fumbled their way into what was the first affair for both of them, more like friends playing than lovers" (Leslie Fiedler, "Nude Croquet").

SHMIGEGGE   See *shmegegge*.

SHMO

Also *schmo* and *shmoe*. Pronounced "shmoh." Perhaps from the Yiddish *schmuck*, "penis." Or perhaps from the Yiddish *shmoo*, "illicit profit." Noun: a boob.

American soldiers in World War II spoke of Joe Schmoe (or Joe Smoe).

The cartoonist Al Capp, creator of the strip "Li'l Abner," coined the name "shmoo" for a hapless, egg-shaped creature that lays eggs, gives milk, tastes like chicken, and enjoys being kicked. Capp said he chose the name because the expressive sounds *sh-* and *m-* suggest the richness of this planet, of which his shmoo creature is a microcosm. "Folks don't need these li'l shmoos!!," Capp wrote in *The Life and Times of the Shmoo* (1948). "They already got one—th' biggest shmoo of all—*th' earth, itself* !! Jest like these li'l shmoos, it's ready t'give ev'rybody ev'rthing they need!!" Many suspect that Capp really got the name from the Yiddish *shmo*.

"He's the *schmo* of the week—52 times a year" (in a poster for the movie *June Bride*, starring Bette Davis and Robert Montgomery).

SHMOCK See *schmuck*.

SHMOE See *shmo*.

SHMOHAWK
Pronounced "SHMOH-hawk." Perhaps from the Yiddish *schmuck*, "penis."
Vulgar (noun): penis.

SHMOOS See *shmooz*.

SHMOOSE See *shmooz*.

SHMOOZ
Also *shmoos, shmoose, shmooze, shmuess,* and *shmus*. From the Hebrew *sh'muoth*, "small talk."
1. Noun: a heart-to-heart talk.
2. Noun: idle talk.
3. Verb: to chitchat.

"It cannot be easy to be a United States congressman. I know it looks easy, all that smiling, *shmoosing*, and striking of historic poses. . . ." (R. Emmett Tayrell, Jr., *The American Spectator*).

"On the Lower East Side, off Third Street, he spoke pidgin Spanish. He played pool. He *schmoozed*" (Marcia Chambers, "Life and Death of a Campus Drug Dealer," *The New York Times*, September 5, 1982).

4. (Garment-worker slang) verb: to talk shop.

SHMOOZE   See *shmooz.*

SHMOTTE   See *schmate.*

SHMUCK   See *schmuck.*

SHMUESS   See *shmooz.*

SHMUS   See *shmooz.*

SHMUTS
Also *shmutz.* The "u" is pronounced like the "ou" in "could." From the German *Schmutz,* "smut" or "dirt."
Noun: Filth; dirt; garbage; smut.

> "*Shmutz* he lives in and I shouldn't worry?" (Philip Roth, *Goodbye Columbus*).

SHMUTZ   See *shmuts.*

SHNAPS
Also *schnaps.* Pronounced "shnahps." From the German *Schnaps,* "spirits" or "brandy."
Noun: liquor.

> "The man's voice greeted him. 'A good awakening to you, Reb Sheftel. Let me have a *schnaps*—my throat's parched. Or Slivovitz —anything will do, as long as I wet whistle'" (Isaac Bashevis Singer, "The Dead Fiddler").

SHNAYDER   See *schneider.*

SHNECKEN   See *schnecken.*

SHNELL
Pronounced "shnell." From the German *schnell,* for "quick."
Adverb: swiftly.
Adjective: quick.

SHNOK   See *shnook.*

SHNOOK
Also *schnook, shnok,* and *shnuk.* Pronounced "shnook."

There is much controversy about the origin. It could be a deriva-
tive of the Yiddish *schmuck,* "penis." Or it could be from the
Yiddish *shnuk,* "snout" or "trunk," which some linguists claim also
suggests the male member. Or it might be from the German
Schnucke, "an undersized sheep," or *Schnucki,* "pet."

1. Noun: a pathetic but lovable fool.

"With *Stir Crazy,* in which he rejoins his *Silver Streak* partner,
Richard Pryor, Gene Wilder proves that he is still America's most
lovable *schnook:* the maniac glint in his blue eyes, the nervous energy
in his movements and the shy, bewildered smile that conveys the
innocent generosity of the eternal adolescent have conspired to
create an image that kindled our collective imagination. (Dan Yakir,
"Gene Wilder: The 'Silver Streak' *Schnook," American Pop*).

In an article on marital problems in *Time* (February 6, 1956), a
husband says, "I'm a poor *shnook.*"

2. (Salesman slang) noun: easy mark; sucker.
3. (English public-school slang) verb: to gesture derisively by putting the
thumb to the nose and extending, or wiggling, the fingers. Used as "to
pull a *shnook.*"

"The custom seems to be one of venerable antiquity and low
origin," writes Morris Murple in *Public School Slang,* "known also
(but not in schools) as *taking a sight, working the coffee-mill, taking
a grinder, pulling bacon, making a long nose* and *making Queen Anne's
fan.* Some of these (e.g. *working the coffee-mill, taking a grinder*)
imply movement of the fingers as well. Emphasis may be added to
the gesture by using both the hands."

4. (English public-school slang) verb: to complete an exam; to outargue
an opponent.

This use of *shnook* was common in the nineteenth century at the
Shrewsbury School, according to J. S. Farmer's *Public School Word-
Book.*

SHNORRER   See *schnorrer.*

SHNOZ

Also *schnozz, schnozzle, schnozzo, schnozzola, shnozzle,* and *shnozzola.* In each case the "oz" is pronounced like the home of the Wizard. From the German *Schnauze,* "snout."

1. Noun: a nose; a huge proboscis.

> "Jimmy Durante was the great *shnozzola.* Meryl Streep has a patrician *shnoz.* And Charles de Gaulle had *le grand shnozzle.*"

> "When you write up da *schnozz,*" said Jimmy Durante, "you better make it 4 inches by 5 inches. I don't wanna start getting the rep of not havin' a big *schnozz*" (W. R. Burnett, *Asphalt Jungle,* 1949).

2. Noun: a long-nosed person.
3. (Underworld patois) noun: an addict who takes drugs only through the nose. The preferred form here is *schnozzler.*

SHNOZZLE   See *shnoz.*

SHNOZZOLA   See *shnoz.*

SHNUK   See *shnook.*

SHOLEM   See *shalom.*

SHOL'M   See *shalom.*

SHOMMES   See *shamus.*

SHONDE   See *shanda.*

SHPIGEL

Pronounced "SHPIG-el." From the German, *Spiegel,* "mirror."
Noun: a mirror.

> Two Yiddish adages: "Everyone sees his best friend in the *shpigel*" and "Only the ugly are fooled by a *shpigel.*"

SHPILKES

Pronounced "SHPILL-kuhs."
Noun: jitters; anxiety; the condition of having ants in one's pants.

This word is part of Calvin Trillin's *shtik*. In June 1982 he told Studs Terkel on a WFMT radio show that "Seventh Avenue *Shpilkes*" is not getting an invitation to a party given by the designer Oscar de la Renta (New York's Seventh Avenue is the heart of the fashion industry). In the June 17, 1981, issue of *The Nation*, however, Trillin wrote that "Seventh Avenue *Shpilkes*" is what Oscar pretends to get when he wants to disinvite an invitee. Trillin explained that the De la Rentas never invite more than one guest of a given occupation so that each guest will feel unique. Once Henry Kissinger was invited, but he declined because of a prior engagement. At the last moment he changed his plans and informed the De la Rentas that he was coming. Mrs. de la Renta, Trillin said, was quite upset because the last-minute addition of Kissinger meant that there would be two war criminals in attendance. "What to do," Trillin wrote, "except to phone the man who conflicts with the star and tell him dinner had to be called off because Mr. d had come down with a painful skin disease known as the Seventh Avenue *Shpilkes*."

A friend knows of an aspiring thespian named Goldie who was supposed to do a skit for her acting class. A week before the performance Goldie told Mary, one of her classmates, that she wouldn't be able to put on the skit on account of *shpilkes*. On the day the performance was scheduled, Goldie was absent and the teacher asked the class if anyone knew why she hadn't shown up. "Goldie's not here," Mary piped up, "because it's a Jewish holiday."

SHTARK

From the German *stark*, "brave," "strong," and "vigorous."
1. Adjective: strong.
2. Noun (*shtarke, shtarker,* or *shtocker*): strong one.

"He slapped Leo on the back. 'Well, how are you doing, *shtarke?*' " (Philip Roth, *Goodbye Columbus*).

"My concept of a *shtarker* is a guy who wears a wool suit without underwear" (Lenny Bruce).

3. Noun (*shtocker*): a strong-arm man; a violent criminal.

"Not a week ago three Gas House *shtockers* stands me up . . . an'
takes me clock" (Alfred Henry Lewis, *Apples of New York*, 1912).

SHTARKE   See *shtark*.

SHTARKER   See *shtark*.

SHTETL
Also *schtetl* and *shtetle*. Pronounced "SHTET-el." From the German
Stadt, "town."
1. Noun: a peasant village of Eastern European Jews.

"He confided to me how, as a strapling of fourteen in Poland
captivated by the Sherlock Holmes stories, he had tailed a putative
malefactor through the streets of their *shtetl*, only to have his quarry,
a harmless chicken-flicker, suddenly whirl around and upbraid him
(S. J. Perelman, *Eastward Ha!*).

"Like most Jewish parents of the *shtetl*, mine wanted their son to
study the violin. Not as a profession, God forbid, nor as a hobby,
simply as part of my education. Like the Talmud, or Latin. It made
a good impression. And it certainly wouldn't hurt" (Elie Wiesel,
"The Violin").

2. Adjective: characteristic of a peasant village.

"But for all that, he has remained the *schtetl* Jew formed by
poverty, family loyalty and Jewish law, and when he discovers Sasa
fornicating with another anarchist he is overwhelmed" (review of
"The Journals of David Toback," *The New York Times Book Review*).

SHTETLE   See *shtetl*.

SHTICK   See *shtik*.

SHTIK
Also *schtick*, *schtik*, and *shtick*. From the German *Stück*, "piece," "bit,"
or "part."
1. Noun: a bit; a piece.

2. Noun: a characteristic mannerism, routine, or gesture, especially of a performer.

> "Richard Simmons, the Sultan of Svelte, Applies Both the Carrot and the *Shtick*" (headline of an article in *People*, November 2, 1981).

> "Do you do that same old *shtik*?" (Steve Allen, in the song "How's Your Sister?").

> "Why do coyotes howl at night?"
> "Cause that's their *shtick*."
> "What he means, in his crude way, hon, is that that's their thing" (Tom K. Ryan, in the cartoon strip "Tumbleweeds").

> "Still the movie is a comedy. Which means that Billy Barty [a three-foot nine-inch actor] has once again gotten the short end of the *schtick*" (New York *Daily News*, August 2, 1981).

SHTIKLE
Pronounced "shtickel." Diminutive form of the Yiddish *shtik*, "a bit" or "a piece."
1. Noun: a little bit; a piece of.

> Some examples: *shtikle dreck* ("a piece of shit"), *shtikle fleysh* ("a piece of meat"), and *shtikle tuches* ("a piece of ass").

> "These ladies," my mother said, "they're now workers for me, not yours. I didn't take them away from you. I just told them I'd treat them like human beings, not like animals. Here by me it's no more a nickel a *shtikle*. You want them back? Pay them more" (Jerome Weidman, *Tiffany Street*).

2. Adjective: a bit of; somewhat of.

> "He's a *shtikle* mathematician" means "He's a bit of a mathematician."

SHTINKEN
Pronounced "SHTINK-en." From the German *stinken*, "to smell foul."
Verb: to stink.

SHTOCKER   See *shtark*.

SHTRAHMEL

Pronounced "SHTRY-mul." From the Polish *stroj*, "fancy dress."
1. Noun: velvet hat worn by Orthodox Jews on special occasions.

"The poles were held up by four *yeshiva buchers*, seminary students from uptown with long side-curls and broad-brimmed *shtrahmels*" (Jerome Weidman, *Fourth Street East*).

2. (Slang) noun: a run-of-the-mill hat.

SHTUNK

Pronounced "shtoonk." From the German *Stunk*, "stink."
1. Noun: something that smells gross.

"The skunk was a *shtunk.*"

2. Noun: an ungrateful jerk.

"George Steinbrenner is a *shtunk.*"

SHTUP

Also *schtup*. The "u" is pronounced like the "ou" in "could." From the German *stupsen*, "to push or shove."
1. Verb: to push; to force something on someone.

"As other children hear the story of Scrooge every year, or are read to nightly from some favorite book, I am continually *shtupped* full of the suspense-filled chapters of her perilous life" (Philip Roth, *Portnoy's Complaint*).

A Yiddish proverb warns us: "The door of success is labeled '*shtup*' and 'pull.'"

2. Verb: to bribe; to tip excessively in a way that is almost like offering a bribe.

"Mrs. Menashim found out, never mind how, that by *shtupping* Gelfman's brother-in-law a ten-dollar bill her Howie could be fixed up in the post office for the summer months" (Wallace Markfield, *Teitlebaum's Window*).

3. (Vulgar) verb: to fuck.

"That's what you get for *schtuppin* the talent, you're stuck" (Daniel Fuchs, *West of the Rockies*).

4. (Vulgar) noun: a female fornicator.

"Hedley Lamarr stood outside the Rock Ridge Saloon, gazing with smug satisfaction at the ornate, gilt-lettered sign, surrounded by blinking gaslights, that read: HEDLEY LAMARR PRESENTS LILI VON SHTUPP, THE TEUTONIC TITWILLOW WHO INVADED THE HEARTS OF EUROPE" (Tad Richards, *Blazing Saddles*, a novel based on the Mel Brooks film).

5. (Vulgar) noun (*schtupper* or *shtupper*): a male fornicator.

"To a Jew *fuck* and *shit* have the same value on the dirty word graph. A Jew has no concept that *fuck* is worth 90 points and *shit* 10. And the reason for that—well, see, rabbis and priests both shit, but only one fucks. . . . And the leaders of my tribe, rabbis, are *schtuppers*, perhaps that's why the words come freer to me" (Lenny Bruce).

6. (Vulgar) noun: the act of sexual intercourse.

SHTUPPER   See *shtup*.

SHTUS   See *shtuss*.

SHTUSS
Also *shtus*. The "u" is pronounced like the "ou" in "could." From a Hebrew word for "ignorance."
1. Noun: nonsense.
2. Noun: an uproar; a fuss.

SHUL
Pronounced "shool." From the German *Schule*, "school."

The derivation is explained by the fact that the synagogue has always served as a place to study as well as to pray.

Noun: a synagogue.

Shlomo was delighted. After thirty years alone on a desolate island in the South Pacific he was finally rescued. He jumped about and cackled with glee as he showed the rescue party all the things he had constructed to make his life more civilized. Shlomo was particularly proud of a *shul* he had made from bamboo sticks and palm leaves. Before departing with them, Shlomo took the rescue party around the entire island. They came across a beautiful synagogue that was identical to the one Shlomo had made. "What's that?," they asked him.

"Oh, *that*," he said, with a contemptuous wave of his hand, "that's the *shul* I wouldn't step foot in."

SHVEBELEH
Pronounced "SHVEH-bel-eh." From the Hebrew.
Noun: a very excitable person.

"The authors' mothers are *shvebelehs* when their sons are driving them around in the family car."

SHVENGERN
Pronounced "SHVENG-urn." From the German *schwangen*, "to be pregnant."
Adjective: pregnant.

SHVINDLE
Also *schwindle*. Pronounced "SHVIN-del." From the German *Schwindel*, "fraud."
Noun: swindle.
Verb: to swindle.

"In fact, he compared himself to Lenin. 'I know,' he said, 'how Lenin felt in October when he exclaimed "*Es schwindelt*!" He didn't mean he was *schwindling* everyone but that he felt giddy' " (Saul Bellow, *Humboldt's Gift*).

SHVINDELDIK
Pronounced "SHVIN-del-dick." From the German *Schwindel*, "vertigo" or "giddiness."
Adjective: dizzy; unsteady.

"My son wants to climb Mt. Everest. Me? I get *shvindeldik* when I step on a stool."

SHVITSER See *shvitzer.*

SHVITZER

Also *shvitser.* Pronounced "SHVITS-er." From the German *schwitzen,* "to sweat."
1. Noun: someone who sweats a lot, especially a nervous seducer.

"First he put one hand on my breast. Then he put his other hand in my ginger ale. Sleep with him? That *shvitzer.* I couldn't even finish my drink."

2. Noun: a braggart.

SHVONTZ

Also *schwanz* and *shvuntz.* Pronounced "shvahnts." From the German *Schwanz,* "tail."
1. Noun: penis.

"A horny unicorn was the only member of its species aboard the Ark. Noah wouldn't let it get off. So it faced the future with its *shvontz* between its legs."

In *Eastward Ha!* S. J. Perelman has an Israeli barber use *schwanz* as if it meant moustache. "You want an advice from a tonsorial engineer? Nobody's got a *schwanz* like yours anymore—it's an antique. Better it should droop around the mouth on both sides."

2. Noun: an ungallant fool.

"[Jack Ruby] yearned to be a *mensch,* a pillar of the community, but always remained a *schwanz*" (obituary in *Time*).

SHVUNTZ See *shvontz.*

SIMCHA

Also *simche* and *simkhe.* Pronounced "SIM-kheh." From the Hebrew *simkha,* "rejoicing."
Noun: a joy; a great pleasure; a celebration.

"THE HUNCHBACK REJOICES IF HE SEES A BIGGER HUMP."

Several Yiddish proverbs indicate that deformed people can have their *simcha*. For example, "The hunchback rejoices if he sees a bigger hump."

SIMCHE   See *simcha*.

SIMKHE   See *simcha*.

SITZFLEISH   See *zitsflaish*.

SZHLOK
Pronounced "zhlock."
Noun: a nincompoop.

> "What a *szhlok* I am!," exclaimed a man who had been talked into buying an ill-fitting suit (Matt Freedman, in the cartoon strip "Free Associates," *The Chicago Reader*).

> In 1955 Shlomo was hit on the head by a falling Torah. He was knocked out and didn't wake up until 1969. The first thing he saw

when he opened his eyes was Old Glory flying at half-mast. "What happened?," he cried out in great distress.

"General Eisenhower just died," replied a bystander.

"Oh, my God," Shlomo cried, "that *szhlok* Nixon is President."

SZLOB   See *zhlub*.

TAM

Pronounced "tom." From the Hebrew *ta'am*, "taste."
1. Noun: taste; appropriateness.

> Good *tam* is champagne in a slipper. Bad *tam* is beer in a boot.

> Good *tam* is "What's black and white and red all over? (Answer: a blushing zebra)." Bad *tam* is "What's black and white and red all over? (Answer: a nun in a Cuisinart)."

> Terrible *tam* is "Why did Menachem Begin invade Lebanon? (Answer: to impress Jodie Foster)."

2. Noun: a simpleton. This meaning comes from the Hebrew *tam*, "simpleton."

TAMAVATEH

Pronounced "TAM-ah-vai-teh." From the Hebrew *tam*, "simpleton." Adjective: dopey.

> "Sure, I'd like a nice Hawaiian punch," said the *tamavateh* lady.

TARARAM   See *tareram*.

TARERAM

Also *tararam*, *tarrarom*, and *terrarom*. Pronounced "teh-ruh-ROM." Noun: hubbub; commotion; uproar.

TARRAROM   See *tareram*.

T.A.T.   See *toches*.

TATA

Also *tate*. Pronounced "TAH-teh."
Noun: dad.

> "I would have been your *tata* if the gorilla hadn't beaten me over the fence."

TATE   See *tata*.

TCHOTCHKE   See *chatchka*.

TEIVEL

Also *teufel* and *teuvel*. Pronounced "TIE-vull." From the German *Teufel*, "devil."
Noun: a devil, or the Devil.

> The *teivel* is the subject of many Yiddish proverbs: "A man is handsome if he is better looking only than the *teivel*" and "If you live with a *teivel*, you become a *teivel*."

TERRAROM   See *tareram*.

TEUFEL   See *teivel*.

TEUVEL   See *teivel*.

T.L.   See *toches*.

TOCHES

Also *tokhes, tokhis, tokis, tokus, tuchis,* and *tuckas*. Pronounced "TAWKH-is." From the Hebrew *tokheth*, "underside."
Noun: rear end.

> "She took the eggs, grapefruit and lettuce out of the refrigerator, an expression of smug superiority on her face. She tossed her head contemptuously at the refrigerator and hit the door with her *tuchis*" (Herbert Selby, Jr., *Requiem for a Dream*).

> A common Yiddish expression is "*toches ahfen tish*" (literally, "buttocks on the table"), which means "put your ass on the line,"

"put up or shut up." The expression is commonly abbreviated T.A.T. or T.O.T. (the English *on* replaces the Yiddish *ahfen*). Norman Lear's production company is called T.A.T.

In furniture-store slang T.O.T. is an expression salesmen use to describe customers who must pay in cash because their credit is shaky.

T.L., an abbreviation for *toches lecher* (literally, "ass licker"), means a sycophant.

TOKHES   See *toches.*

TOKHIS   See *toches.*

TOKIS   See *toches.*

TOKUS   See *toches.*

T.O.T.   See *toches.*

TRAIF   See *trayf.*

TRAIFNYAK   See *traif.*

TRAYF
Also *traif* and *tref.* From the Hebrew *tref,* "torn to pieces," especially by an animal.
1. Adjective: nonkosher.

"Besides: all right, yourself you can do whatever you want: you can eat *tref,* desecrate the Sabbath, shave your chin—but do you have to blacken your father's face in the Other World?" (J. Ayalti, "The Presence Is in Exile, Too").

A Yiddish folk saying: "If you examine carefully enough, everything is *trayf.*"

2. Noun (*traifnyak*): a despicable individual.

TREF   See *trayf.*

TRIPPER
From the German *Tripper*, "gonorrhea" or "clap."
Noun: gonorrhea.

"Even troopers get *tripper*."

TROMBENIK
Pronounced "TROM-be-nick." From the Polish *tromba*, "brass horn."
1. Noun: a boaster; someone who blows his own horn.

"The gaudy militarism of the portly *trombenik* was more Germanic than Jewish, and at least one newsman had fortuitously spied in Kissinger a puerile compulsion for 'Teuton his own horn'" (Joseph Heller, *Good As Gold*).

2. Noun: a mooch; a freeloader.
3. Noun: a fraud.

TSADIK   See *tzadik*.

TSATSKA   See *chatchka*.

TSATSKALA   See *chatchka*.

TSATSKE   See *chatchka*.

TSEDRAIT
Also *tsedraydelt* and *tsedrayt*. Pronounced "tse-DREIGHT." From the German *drehen*, "to twist."
1. Adjective: "twisted"; kooky.
2. Noun (*tsedrayteh*): a female kook.
3. Noun (*tsedrayter*): a male kook.

TSEDRAYDELT   See *tsedrait*.

TSEDRAYT   See *tsedrait*.

TSEDRAYTEH   See *tsedrait*.

TSEDRAYTER   See *tsedrait*.

TSIMMES

Also *tzimmes*. Pronounced "TSIM-mess."
1. Noun: fuss.

> "He said we had to keep it dark for a month, till he finished Harvard, and then he would stage a big ceremony in Cawnpone, with painted elephants and sword swallowers and the whole *tzimmas*" (S. J. Perelman, "Are You Decent, Memsahib?").

2. Noun: a sweet carrot or turnip compote.

> "Ah, if he could return to his old home and old days, and have his father recite Sanctification again, and sit by his side, opposite to mother and receive from her hand a plate of reeking *tzimmes*, as of yore" (Abraham Cahan, *Yekl*, 1896).

TSITSER

Pronounced "TSIT-sir."
Noun: someone who says "ts! ts!" a lot; a bystander who commiserates but offers no real help.

TSORES

Also *tsoriss, tsouris, tsuris, tsuriss,* and *tzures*. Pronounced "TSOOR-us."
From the Hebrew *tzarah*, "trouble."
Noun: troubles; woes; afflictions; problems.

> *Tsores* afflicts such Yiddish proverbs, as in "When you're dead, you're eaten by worms; when you're alive you're eaten by *tsores*" and "It's better to have *tsores* with soup than without."

> "I call it the *Tsouris* Diet . . . worry is excellent for losing weight," said Eugenia Zukerman, flutist and wife of the violinist Pinchas Zukerman (Princess Ira von Furstenberg, "Eugenia: Slim on *Tsouris* Diet," *New York Post*, July 4, 1981).

TSORISS   See *tsores*.

TSOURIS   See *tsores*.

TSURIS   See *tsores*.

TSURISS See *tsores.*

TSUTUMELT
Pronounced "tsoo-TOO-melt." From the German *tummeln,* "to romp about," "to scuffle."
Adjective: disoriented; dizzy.

TUCHIS See *toches.*

TUCKAS See *toches.*

TUMMEL
Pronounced "TOO-mel." From the German *Tummel,* "scuffle."
Noun: a commotion.

TUSH
Pronounced "tush." From the Yiddish *toches,* "rear end."
Noun: an affectionate word for the rear end.

"My most intense observation [about preppies], though, was of my roommate, Thatcher Baxter Hatcher (nickname: *Tush*), and his sister—whose real name, of course, was not Caca but Baxter Thatcher Hatcher" (Calvin Trillin, *The Nation,* February 7, 1981).

"Buddy minced through the steps with that special flair that was all his own, hands pushing, *tush* wagging, singing in a clear, pouting tenor: 'THROW OUT YOUR HANDS/STICK OUT YOUR TUSH/HANDS ON YOUR HIPS/GIVE 'EM A PUSH' " (Tad Richards, *Blazing Saddles,* a novel based on the Mel Brooks film).

"Here are some panties from my nubile young *tush* " (from a plug on WLS-FM in Chicago for women's underwear that men can buy and sniff).

TUSHIE
Pronounced "tushy." From the Yiddish *toches,* "rear end."
Noun: kids' talk for rear end.

TZADDIK See *tzadik.*

TZADIK

Also *tsadik* and *tzaddik*. Pronounced "TSAH–dick." From the Hebrew *tsadik*, "holy man."

1. Noun: a pious person.

> "For this," Monte says bitterly, "I hired the best *schneiders* ['tailors']. For this I bought the best cloth. For this I chose buttons like they were diamonds. For this I made a suit only a *tzaddik* should wear. So his father should stand there in front of me and say ten dollars" (Jerome Weidman, *Fourth Street East*).

> "In the beginning I saw him as a *tzaddik* in disguise, a saintly sage whose mission it was to gather sparks and wandering souls to unite them with the original flame, the flame that links the Creator to His creation" (Elie Wiesel, *One Generation After*).

2. (Sarcastic) noun: wicked old man, especially one who is a tightwad as well.

TZIMMES   See *tsimmes*.

TZURES   See *tsores*.

U

UMGEDULDIK

Pronounced "OOM-ge-dull-dick." From the German *Ungeduld,* "petulance," "impatience."
Adjective: petulant.

UMMEGLICK

Pronounced "OOM-meg-lech." From the German *unmöglich,* "impossible."
Adjective: extremely unlikely.

UNGEPACHKIT

Pronounced "OON-ge-pach-kit."
Adjective: cluttered.

UNTERSHMEICHLEN

Pronounced "OON-ter-shmice-len." From the German *schmeicheln,* "to butter up," "to flatter."
Verb: to butter up.

UTZ

Pronounced "oots." From the German *uzen,* "to mock," "to tease," "to chaff."
Verb: to needle; to nag.

VAI

Also *weh*. Pronounced "vay." From the German *Weh*, "ache," "misery," "travail," or "grief."
1. Exclamation: pain. Heard in the familiar lament "Oy *vai*."
2. Noun (*vaitik*): a pain.

VAITIK   See *vai*.

VANE   See *vonneh*.

VANTZ

Pronounced "vonts." From the German *Wanze*, "bedbug."
1. Noun: a bedbug.
2. Noun: an inconsequential person; a nobody.

VAYB   See *veib*.

VEIB

Also *vayb*. Pronounced "vibe." From the German *Weib*, "wife."
Noun: a wife.

The truth about the *veib* is captured by more Yiddish proverbs. For example, "If the *veib* wears pants, the husband washes the floors" and "Rain drives you into the house and a nasty *veib* drives you out."

VERLIEREN

Pronounced "fear-LEAR-en." From the German *verlieren*, "to lose." (Garment-worker slang) verb: to lose a customer to a fellow salesman.

VITZ

Pronounced "vits." From the German *Witz*, "joke" or "wit."
Noun: a joke.

> "I was, I remember, a bit piqued at the thought that it was a colleague and not I who had made such a good crack before dying, so I tried to think of an even better *vitz*, but they had already started shooting us, so I had to make do with a visual effect, showing the Germans my *tuchis*" (Romain Gary, "The Dance of Genghis Cohn").

VITZEL

Pronounced "VITS-el." From the German *Witz*, "joke" or "wit."
Noun: a philosophical witticism.

VONNEH

Also *vane*. Pronounced "VA-nah."
Noun: a bath; a bathtub.

> " 'White enamel bathtub with a long slope at one end and four metal claw feet.' In 1927, however, at least on East Fourth Street, the *vonneh* to Mr. Velvel Schmidt's tenants was a spectacular innovation" (Jerome Weidman, *Last Respects*).

VUND

Pronounced "voond." From the German *Wunde*, "wound."
Noun: a wound.

VYZOSO

Pronounced "VAY-zo-so." From the name of an enemy of the Jews in the Book of Esther.
1. Noun: an idiot; a dolt.
2. (Vulgar) noun: penis.

YACHNEH

Also *yakhne*. Pronounced "YOCK-neh."
Noun: a shrew; a loud woman.

YAHUDI   See *yehudi*.

YAKHNE   See *yachneh*.

YEHUDI

Also *yahudi*. Pronounced "ya-HOO-dee." From the Hebrew.
Noun: a Jew.

"His short sojourn in Berlin de-Russianized him completely, and for the rest of his life he behaved toward the despised 'Polacks' with the pomp and condescending airs of the *Yahudi*" (S. L. Blumenson, "From the American Scene: The Politicians," *Commentary*, March 1956).

"What are four things that suggest that Jesus was a *Yehudi*? (Answer: He lived at home until he was thirty. He went into his father's business. His mother thought he was God. And he thought she was a virgin.)"

YENTA

Also *yente* and *yenteh*. Pronounced "YEN-tah."

Yente was originally a woman's name. The notoriety of Yente Telebende, a character in a humor column in the *Jewish Daily Forward*, has reinforced the negative connotations of *yenta* and has made it now virtually impossible for Jews to name their daughters Yente.

1. Noun: a blabbermouth; a nag.

"*Yenta-gram!!* So who can deliver guilt like a nagging *yenta*?? Have our *yentas* personally deliver a *yentagram* guilt-trip to a friend, lover, boss on any occasion. So why haven't you called yet?? The phone is broken??" (classified ad in *The Village Voice,* September 30–October 6, 1981).

"Hollywood's '*yentas*' have predicted disaster for Barbra Streisand's forthcoming movie, 'Yentl' " (*Newsday,* March 16, 1982).

"Dr. Hammerschmidt [a scientist who purportedly discovered that Chinese food prevents heart attacks], I figure, wanted to show up these pure-food *yentas* once and for all so he could enjoy his shredded spiced pork with green peppers in peace—and the rest is medical history" (Calvin Trillin, *The Nation,* June 28, 1980).

A *yenta* is not a matchmaker. This is a mistake occasionally made by the *goyim* because *Yente* is the name of the matchmaker in *Fiddler on the Roof.* A United States Supreme Court justice committed this malapropism: "I'm the *yenta* of Paradise Valley," said Justice Sandra Day O'Connor. "I have introduced a number of couples, including my own sister and brother-in-law" (*Ladies' Home Journal,* March 1982).

2. Verb: to badger.

"How will it look on my gravestone: 'Here lies Lester Pearlman, *yented* to death' " (from the record *The Jewish American Princess*).

YENTE   See *yenta.*

YENTEH   See *yenta.*

YENTZEN
Pronounced "YENTS-en." From the German.
1. Verb: to fuck; to whore.
2. Verb: to "screw"; to swindle.
3. Noun (*yentzer*): someone who sleeps around a lot; a slut.
4. Noun (*yentzer*): a con man.
5. (Underworld patois) noun (*yentzer*): a cheater.

YENTZER See *yentzen.*

YID

Pronounced "yid." From the Hebrew.
(Vulgar) noun: a Jew. At one time the word simply meant "a Jew," without any negative connotations.

YOLD

Pronounced "yeld." From the Hebrew *yeled*, "child."
Noun: a dope; a half-wit.

ZAFTIG

Also *saftig, zaftik,* and *zophtic.* Pronounced "ZOFF-tick." From the German *saftig,* "juicy," "luscious," or "succulent."
Adjective: juicy, plump, and sexy.

> "A decade in Hollywood, luckily, had inured me to *zaftig* female epidermis en masse, and so, if I had nothing better to do—which was rare—I strolled into the wings and allowed the coryphées to cosset me" (S. J. Perelman, "Samson Shorn, or The Slave of Love").

> "As he was being led to his first display case of the day, a seminar in the postwar American novel, a *zaftig* woman in a purple catsuit accosted him by the chapel" (John Updike, *Bech: A Book*).

> "Flossie is a bright, attractive woman, *saftig,* well-organized." (Tom Wolfe, "The Last American Hero," *The Kandy-Kolored Tangerine-Flake Streamline Baby*).

ZAFTIK   See *zaftig.*

ZHLOB   See *zhlub.*

ZHLUB

Also *dzhlob, shlub, shlubbo, shluhb, szlob,* and *zhlob.*
Pronounced "zlub." From the Slavic.
1. Noun: someone who is insensitive and uncouth.
2. Adjective (*zhlubby*): boorish; Gothlike.

> "Even the Kismet Inn, a classic tie-up and tie-on booze station for the *zhlubby* middle-aged boat owners from the other side . . . has now become a swinging singles bar" (Albert Goldman, "I Have Seen the Future—and It's Fire Island," *New York,* June 24, 1972).

ZITSFLAISH

Also *sitzfleish*. Pronounced "ZITS-flysh." From the German *sitzen*, "to sit," and *Fleisch*, "flesh" or "meat." Literally, "sitting meat."

1. Noun: patience; endurance.
2. Noun: buttocks.

> "Apart from having his *sitzfleish* peppered with buckshot, I don't suppose he sustained any actual damage from the shotgun blasts I heard, but he seemed much more subdued thereafter" (S. J. Perelman, "If a Slicker Meets a Slicker").

ZOPHTIC   See *zaftig*.

BIBLIOGRAPHY

BOOKS

Allen, Woody. *Getting Even.* New York: Warner Books, 1972.

Apple, Max. *Zip.* New York: The Viking Press, 1978.

Ausubel, Nathan, ed. *A Treasury of Jewish Humor.* New York: Paperback Library, Inc., 1967.

Azbel, Mark Ya. *Refusenik: Trapped in the Soviet Union.* Boston: Houghton Mifflin, 1981.

Bellow, Saul. *The Adventures of Augie March.* New York: The Viking Press, 1953.

————. *Herzog.* New York: The Viking Press, 1964.

————. *Humboldt's Gift.* New York: The Viking Press, 1975.

————. *To Jerusalem and Back.* New York: The Viking Press, 1976.

————. *Mr. Sammler's Planet.* New York: The Viking Press, 1970.

————. *The Victim.* New York: Vanguard Press, 1947.

Birmingham, Stephen. *"Our Crowd": The Great Jewish Families of New York.* New York: Harper & Row, 1967.

Cahan, Abraham. *Yekl.* New York: D. Appleton & Co., 1896.

Capp, Al. *The Life and Times of the Shmoo.* New York: Holt, Rinehart & Winston, 1948.

Crypton, Dr. *Dr. Crypton and His Problems.* New York: St. Martin's Press, 1982.

Dickens, Charles. *Bleak House.* 1853. (See the 1978 Norton Critical Edition, New York: W. W. Norton & Company, for an authoritative and annotated text.)

Ephron, Nora. *Crazy Salad.* New York: Alfred A. Knopf, 1975.

Feinsilver, Lillian Mermin. *The Taste of Yiddish.* South Brunswick, N.J.: A. S. Barnes & Company, 1970.

Fiedler, Leslie. *The Second Stone.* New York: Stein & Day, 1963.

Freedman, Matt, and Paul Hoffman, *How Many Zen Buddhists Does It Take to Screw in a Lightbulb?* New York: St. Martin's Press, 1980.

Freud, Sigmund. *Jokes and Their Relation to the Unconscious*. New York: W. W. Norton & Company, 1960.

Heller, Joseph. *Good As Gold*. New York: Pocket Books, 1971.

London, Jack. *The Road*. 1907. (See the 1978 edition published by Peregrine Smith, Layton, Utah.)

McGinniss, Joe. *The Selling of the President 1968*. New York: Simon & Schuster, 1969.

Malamud, Bernard. *The Assistant*. New York: New American Library, 1958.

———. *The Tenants*. New York: Pocket Books, 1971.

Markfield, Wallace. *To an Early Grave*. New York: Simon & Schuster, 1964.

———. *Teitlebaum's Window*. New York: Alfred A. Knopf, 1970.

Nabokov, Vladimir. *Lolita*. New York: G. P. Putnam's Sons, 1955.

Nizer, Louis. *The Implosion Conspiracy*. New York: Doubleday & Co., 1975.

Novak, William, and Moshe Waldoks. *The Big Book of Jewish Humor*. New York: Harper & Row, 1981.

Perelman, S. J. *Crazy Like a Fox*. New York: Vintage Books, 1973.

———. *Eastward Ha!* New York: Simon & Schuster, 1977.

Potok, Chaim. *The Chosen*. New York: Simon & Schuster, 1967.

———. *The Promise*. New York: Alfred A. Knopf, 1969.

Roth, Henry. *Call It Sleep*. Totowa, N. J.: Cooper Square Publishers, Inc., 1934.

Roth, Philip. *Goodbye Columbus and Five Short Stories*. Cleveland: The World Publishing Company, 1960.

———. *The Great American Novel*. New York: Holt, Rinehart & Winston, 1973.

———. *Portnoy's Complaint*. New York: Random House, 1969.

Selby, Hubert, Jr. *Last Exit to Brooklyn*. New York: Grove Press, 1957.

———. *Requiem for a Dream*. New York: Playboy Press, 1979.

Simpson, Eileen. *Poets in Their Youth*. New York: Random House, 1982.

Styron, William. *Sophie's Choice*. New York: Random House, 1979.

Turner, Lana. *Lana: The Lady, the Legend, the Truth*. New York: E. P. Dutton, 1982.

Updike, John. *Bech: A Book*. New York: Alfred A. Knopf, 1965.

Weidman, Jerome. *Fourth Street East*. New York: Random House, 1970.

———. *Last Respects*. New York: Random House, 1971.

———. *Tiffany Street*. New York: Random House, 1974.

Wiesel, Elie. *One Generation After*. New York: Random House, 1970.

Wolfe, Tom. "The Last American Hero," *The Kandy-Kolored Tangerine-Flake Streamline Baby*. New York: Farrar, Straus & Giroux, 1965.

Wolff, Geoffrey. *The Duke of Deception*. New York: Berkley Books, 1969.
Zangwill, Israel. *Children of the Ghetto*. New York, 1892.
————. *Dreams of the Ghetto*. New York: Harper & Brothers, 1898.

SHORT STORIES

Bellow, Saul. "The Old System" and "The Old People," *Mosby's Memoirs and Other Stories*. New York: The Viking Press, 1968.
Cahan, Abraham. "The Imported Bridegroom," *The Imported Bridegroom and Other Stories of the New York Ghetto*. New York: Houghton Mifflin, 1898.
Chandler, Raymond. "Farewell, My Lovely," *The Raymond Chandler Omnibus*. New York: Alfred A. Knopf, 1964.
Dick, Isaac Meier. "Two Strangers Came to Town," *A Treasury of Jewish Humor*. New York: Paperback Library, 1967.
Fiedler, Leslie. "Nobody Ever Died from It" and "Nude Croquet," *Pull Down Vanity and Other Stories*. Philadelphia: J. B. Lippincott Company, 1948.
Gary, Romain. "The Dance of Genghis Cohn," *The Big Book of Jewish Humor*. New York: Harper & Row, 1981.
Gold, Michael. "Sam Kravitz, That Thief," *Jews Without Money*. New York: Liveright Publishing Company, 1930.
Malamud, Bernard. "The Last Mohican" and "The Jewbird," *The Magic Barrel*. New York: Farrar, Straus & Cudahy, 1958.
Nadir, Moishe. "My First Deposit," *A Treasury of Jewish Humor*. New York: Paperback Library, 1967.
Roth, Philip. "The Conversion of the Jews," "Eli, the Fanatic," and "Epstein," *Goodbye Columbus and Five Short Stories*. Cleveland: The World Publishing Company, 1960.
Singer, I. B. "Advice," "The Dead Fiddler," "Fire," "The Lecture," and "The Needle," *The Seance and Other Stories*. New York: Farrar, Straus & Giroux, 1968.
————. "A Piece of Advice," *The Spinoza of Market Street*. New York: Farrar, Straus & Cudahy, 1958.
Vonnegut, Kurt, Jr. "The Hyannis Port Story," *Welcome to the Monkey House*. New York: Dell Publishing Company, 1970.

MAGAZINES

American Pop

The American Spectator

American Speech

Atlantic Monthly

Commentary

Family Weekly

Games

Inside Sports

Kirkus Reviews

Ladies' Home Journal

Mad

The Nation

The National Observer

New Republic

New York

New York *Sunday News Magazine*

The New York Review of Books

The New York Times Book Review

The New York Times Magazine

The New Yorker

Newsweek

People

Playboy

Playgirl

Rolling Stone

Saturday Review

Time

Variety

NEWSPAPERS

The Boston Globe

The Boston Herald American

The Chicago Reader

The Daily Herald

Daily News

The Harvard Crimson

Jewish Daily Forward

Jewish Guardian

The Lincoln (Nebraska) *Evening Journal*

New York Daily News

The New York Daily Worker

New York Evening Post

New York Post

The New York Times

Newsday

The Wall Street Journal   *The Village Voice*
The Washington Post

MOVIES

Animal Crackers   *June Bride*
Battery Battalion   *Last Tango in Paris*
Blazing Saddles   *No Way to Treat a Lady*
Bowery Battalion   *Robin and the Seven Hoods*
The Competition   *Sleeper*